the complete

Residential Property Investment

in New Zealand

the complete guide to

Residential Property Investment

in **New Zealand**

Lisa Dudson & Andrew King

RANDOM HOUSE
NEW ZEALAND

National Library of New Zealand Cataloguing-in-Publication Data
Dudson, Lisa.
The complete guide to residential property investment in New Zealand /
Lisa Dudson and Andrew King.
ISBN 1-86941-562-0
1. Real estate investment—New Zealand. 2. Rental housing—New
Zealand. I. King, Andrew (Andrew Martin Duncan) II. Title.
332.63240993—dc 21

A RANDOM HOUSE BOOK
published by
Random House New Zealand
18 Poland Road, Glenfield, Auckland, New Zealand
www.randomhouse.co.nz

First published 2003, reprinted 2003

ISBN 1 86941 562 0

Text design: Graeme Leather
Cover design: Katy Yiakmis
Printed by Griffin Press, Australia

Contents

Disclaimer

The information contained in this book is given in good faith and has been derived from sources believed to be accurate at the date of issue. No liability will be accepted by the authors or publishers for actions taken by any person on the strength of this information alone.

This material is not to be published without prior written consent from Lisa Dudson or Andrew King.

It is recommended that independent advice be sought.

Introduction

Congratulations on purchasing *The Complete Guide to Residential Property Investment in New Zealand*. We believe this will be a significant step on your road to financial freedom through property investment.

The guide was developed because there are limited comprehensive, independent educational services available to residential property investors. We often come across people who have jumped into property investment without really knowing what they are doing.

If you ask the professionals who work with them how many property investors really know what they are doing, you get an answer of around 5 to 10%. So that leaves a large number who could do a lot better. Often small changes can lead to significant differences to the bottom line.

Property is an investment that has proven very popular with New Zealanders. Currently, there are approximately 170,000 property investors in the country. The average investor owns only one or two properties – only 9% own more than two properties. It is an investment that offers the opportunity to create significant wealth. Although the current low inflation environment makes it slightly more difficult, there are still plenty of opportunities to create wealth through property investment, but you need to be a little smarter about how you do it.

As one of the largest industries in New Zealand, property investment is a business and should be treated as such. This involves spending the time to educate yourself on how to run that business efficiently, professionally and, most importantly, profitably.

This guide provides an overview of the information you need to be a successful property investor. However, it is no substitute for good professional advice. We cannot stress strongly enough how important it is to get good advice from someone who specialises in property investment.

This book has been compiled with the help of a number of experts. We would like to thank Scotney Williams, Williams Consultancy; Dale Smith, accountant; Kelvin Mackie, Skeates Simpsom Dowsett; Steve Tucker, Valuit Asset Appraisals; Chris Bridgeman, EZIHome; Maurice Ridge, Shoreinsurance; Keith Knarston, McKay Knarston; and Steve Dunlop, Dunlop Stewart.

We wish you well and trust you will get tremendous value out of our guide.

If you have any ideas on how we can improve this guide we would be grateful for your feedback. You can contact us at lisa.dudson@acumen.co.nz or andrew@propertyinvestor.info.

Lisa Dudson and Andrew King

1

How Property Investment Works: An Overview

Investment in property can be achieved in two ways: acquiring a property with the aim of renting it out, and buying or building a property with the aim of selling it for a profit on completion.

In the first case, you are a property investor and in the second you are a property developer. A key difference between investor and developer is how each is taxed for capital gains. An investor is primarily seeking rental income, and any capital gain (increase in the property's value) is not taxed. A developer is primarily making an income through capital enhancement, and therefore capital gains are taxed.

It is important to decide at an early stage what you are going to do so that you are correctly designated for tax purposes. If you are a developer as well as a property investor, your rental property is tainted by your development property — which means you will have to pay capital gains tax on your rental properties should you sell them. Forming trusts and companies or investing through partners, friends or relatives is unlikely to help as the Inland Revenue Department (IRD) will claim that you were associated with these people. (This is a hint to keep an eye on what your business associates and close relations are up to and how you are linked to them. You could end up being tainted by default.)

In this book we focus on long-term residential property investment. Here, we provide an overview of residential property investment, and explain important topics in detail in the following sections.

Making money through investment property

There are two key ways to make money from an investment property: through excess rental income over expenditure, and through capital growth.

The ideal investment property is one that has a high rental return, low outgoings and high capital growth. Unfortunately, these goals are usually inversely proportionate to one another.

Rental yield

Not all properties produce the same rental yields. It can be difficult to get high rental returns in high growth areas. As a general rule, the rental yield for properties goes down as the price of properties goes up. For instance, a $100,000 property may rent for $160 a week, giving it a yield of 8.3%. However, this does not mean that a $300,000 property will rent for $480. The higher priced property may rent for $300 per week and only provide a 5.2% yield. (An equation for comparing rental returns is the gross rental yield. This is calculated by dividing the annual rental return by the price of the property and multiplying that sum by 100. This way you can compare the rental yields from two different properties with markedly different values and rental returns.)

Because cheaper properties often have higher rental yields than expensive properties, they tend to make better investments. Using the above example, it would be better to purchase three $100,000 properties than one $300,000 property. Weekly rentals from the three properties would be $480 compared with $300 for the more expensive property.

When looking to buy property, you should focus on buying in areas where you believe house prices will rise by more than the national average – and where you have greater opportunity for high capital growth. But because these areas may not provide a high rental yield, you may need to enhance the property to improve the rental return you receive from it.

Novice property investors often overlook the effect outgoings can have on net rental return. Outgoings that are easily overlooked include maintenance costs, vacancy rates, council rate payments, insurance premiums and body corporate fees. Different property types and locations can affect the size of these outgoings.

Capital gains

The second form of income for the property investor is capital gains. This is often where the real money is made in property. However, it can take time to achieve.

The factor that can accelerate your investment return is leverage. Leverage is purchasing rental property using borrowed money instead of your own. The higher the amount you borrow, the more you are said to be leveraged.

If your property goes up in value, then the more you are leveraged, the higher the return on the actual money you have invested. This is demonstrated in the following chart, which shows the different returns achieved on the same property, bought 20 years ago for $60,000, with different borrowing levels. The loan is interest only at a rate of 8%. As you can see, the return on the actual money invested (the internal rate of return) is highest with the highest level of borrowing.

Purchase price	$60,000	$60,000	$60,000	$60,000
% borrowed against purchase price	0	40	75	90
Actual investment	**$60,000**	**$36,000**	**$15,000**	**$6,000**
Rental income over 20 years	$90,000	$90,000	$90,000	$90,000
Mortgage payments over 20 years (at 8% interest)	($0)	($38,400)	($72,000)	($86,400)
Net income over 20 years	$90,000	$51,600	$18,000	$3,600
Value after 20 years @ 5% p.a.	$159,198	$159,198	$159,198	$159,198
Capital gain after 20 years (Current value – purchase price)	$99,198	$99,198	$99,198	$99,198
Total return over 20 years (Net income + capital gain)	$189,198	$150,798	$117,198	$102,798
Average annual return on investment	**16%**	**21%**	**39%**	**86%**

• brackets ( ) indicate a negative figure.

The advantage of borrowing is that it can allow you to buy more properties than if you didn't borrow. Consider the situation outlined on page 16. Say 20 years ago you had $60,000, which was then sufficient to buy one rental property without a mortgage. If you borrowed 75% of the purchase price instead of paying it all in your own cash, you could then afford to buy four rental properties. Over time, this can work out better financially.

Of course, having no mortgage means no mortgage interest payments and no outstanding debt. However, over a long-term period capital gain increases may achieve much higher overall returns to the investor. Consider the following chart comparing the purchase of one property 20 years ago for $60,000 cash and four similar properties with 75% mortgages. The figures assume an average growth rate of 5% per annum, a gross rental yield of 7.5% and average interest rates of 8%. Even with the mortgage payments and a continuing debt, the investor is still better off by borrowing to buy more property. However, this will include extra management time. This example doesn't take account of potential tax advantages, which would make the four-property option even more attractive.

	1 property	4 properties
Property value after 20 years	$159,198	$636,791
Rental income over 20 years	$90,000	$360,000
Interest-only mortgage payments	$0	($288,000)
Outstanding debt	$0	($180,000)
Net worth after 20 years	$249,198	$528,791

However, there is a risk to high borrowing if property values fall: then leverage works in reverse. In other words, it accelerates your losses.

High levels of leveraging can also leave you exposed to interest rate rises that could see you unable to finance your mortgage commitments. Many investors who buy rental property when interest rates are low do not consider the ramifications of interest rate rises. Such rate rises can see the investor forced to sell the rental property, which is never a good thing to have to do. The risks of high borrowing are further explained in 'Risk Analysis' (see pages 64–68).

The importance of capital growth

Although you may have contributed little or nothing of your own money to purchase a property, as the owner you get the benefit of any increase in its capital value.

Capital growth and leveraging play a large part in increasing your Internal Rate of Return (IRR). The IRR is a calculation that shows the return based on the actual amount you have invested. It is calculated by combining the net profit from rental income with capital gains, dividing this figure by the actual amount you have invested (usually your deposit), and multiplying this sum by 100. This figure shows your actual return on money invested and can then be used to compare this investment with others on the same basis.

The point to remember is that if the property is worth $200,000 and increases in value (capital growth) by 5%, then you get the benefit of the whole $10,000 increase in value – regardless of how much money you invested yourself. For instance, if you invested

$20,000 in the property, your return is not just 5% of the $20,000 deposit; you get 5% of the entire property's value, or $10,000 in this case. This means that the IRR on your investment is actually 50%.

Leveraging your investment can certainly dramatically increase the return on your property investment. However, you should be aware that there is a sting in its tail.

Just as leveraging increases your return when the property goes up in value, it also increases the loss should the property go down in value. Using the above example, if the $200,000 property went down in value by 5%, then you would have made a 50% loss on your $20,000 investment.

This is why it is important to buy property in a location where you expect higher than average capital gains (which could be due to many reasons such as a good local economy, increasing population, low supply of land for new development, etc).

You make money with property investments when you buy a property. This means buying wisely: in a location that has potential for improvement, provides a high yield, and can be purchased at a reduced (wholesale) price or has the ability to make improvements that increase the value of the property.

The best way to increase the property value is to increase the rent. This has the double advantage of increasing income as well. The best way to increase the rent is to add features that tenants desire and are willing to pay for. Examples are a garage or carport, extra bedroom (adding onto the building, reorganising existing rooms, or adding a sleepout), carpet, fence, security alarm and whiteware. Just making the place clean and tidy can give you a price advantage over other rental properties. Improvements are best considered (and budgeted for) before purchasing the property.

When adding value, make sure the extra cost will achieve a high return on your investment. Adding a second-hand washing machine, dryer and fridge may cost $1000 but can lead to a rent increase of $20 per week. This equates to a 100% return on your $1000 investment after the first year, so would be well worth doing.

Control

As a property investor, you have control over most parts of your investment.

✓ You decide if the purchase price, rental yield and potential for capital growth are acceptable and how much cash you are going to put in, if any.

✓ You decide which lender to go to for finance and how you will structure the borrowings.

✓ You decide if and how you are going to improve the property's value and its rental income to achieve the rental return that you want.

✓ You decide if you will manage the property yourself or pay a manager to do it for you.

✓ You decide how you are going to maintain the property and whether you will repair it yourself (if you can) or get someone else to do it.

✓ You must be knowledgeable about and consider factors that are out of your control, such as interest rates, rental and housing market changes, and decide on how you are going to deal with these factors.

You are in control, which is great. But the responsibility to make sure it works is also with you. Consider yourself the managing director of your property investments, even if your empire amounts to a small one-bedroom flat. By acknowledging that you are in charge, and accepting the responsibility for success or failure, you will be more likely to seek out good information and take your investment seriously.

This doesn't mean you have to undertake everything yourself, but it does mean that you have to take an interest in exactly what is going on. Residential property is not a passive investment.

Investment property example

Following is a cashflow example of how an investment property may work out over a five-year period. The property in this example consists of two brick-and-tile flats with two bedrooms in each dwelling, and aluminium joinery. The gross rental yield is 9.5%. The property was purchased for $220,000 with a 20% deposit. This is an older property with chattels (carpet, whiteware, etc) valued at only $20,000. The mortgage interest rate is 7.5% fixed for five years, paying interest only.

The inflation rate is estimated to average 2.5% a year and property values are assumed to increase in line with inflation. (According to Statistics New Zealand information, house prices have risen around one percentage point more than general inflation over the past 30 years.) This example does not allow for a property manager. If you are going to use a property manager allow 7.5% of rental income to cover the fees.

As this is a low-maintenance property, only 5% of the rental income is allocated to repairs and maintenance. A two-week

Five-year property analysis

	Year 1	Year 2	Year 3	Year 4	Year 5
Property value	$220,000	$225,500	$231,138	$236,916	$242,839
Building value	$110,000	$105,600	$101,376	$97,321	$93,428
Chattels value	$20,000	$17,600	$15,488	$13,629	$11,994
Deposit / investment	$44,000	$44,000	$44,000	$44,000	$44,000
Mortgage interest rate %	7.5	7.5	7.5	7.5	7.5
Weekly rent	$400	$410	$420	$431	$442
Inflation rate %	2.5	2.5	2.5	2.5	2.5
Rental yield %	9.5	9.7	9.9	10.2	10.4
Annual rent	$20,800	$21,320	$21,840	$22,412	$22,984
Annual interest-only mortgage payment	$13,200	$13,200	$13,200	$13,200	$13,200
Insurance	$360	$369	$378	$388	$397
Rates	$1,500	$1,538	$1,576	$1,615	$1,656
Property manager	$0	$0	$0	$0	$0
Other	$500	$513	$525	$538	$552

Maintenance at 5% of rental income	$1,040	$1,066	$1,092	$1,121	$1,149
2 week vacancy provision	$800	$820	$840	$862	$884
Total expenses	$17,400	$17,506	$17,611	$17,724	$17,838
Chattels depreciation claim (assumed 12% average allowance)	$2,400	$2,112	$1,859	$1,636	$1,439
Building depreciation claim (4%)	$4,400	$4,224	$4,055	$3,893	$3,737
Tax refund / payable (assuming a 33% tax rate)	($1,122)	($832)	($556)	($277)	($10)
Cash loss / gain (rent – expenses + tax refund)	$4,522	$4,646	$4,785	$4,965	$5,156
Capital gain (property value x inflation)	$5,500	$5,638	$5,778	$5,923	$6,071
Profit (not including building depreciation)	$8,174	$8,541	$8,918	$9,334	$9,756
Internal rate of return %	18.58	19.41	20.27	21.21	22.17
Gross value of investment (Includes cash loss/gain)	$54,022	$59,784	$65,701	$71,804	$78,066
Building depreciation & 50% of chattels depreciation clawed back by IRD	($1,848)	($3,590)	($5,235)	($6,790)	($8,260)
Real estate agent fees	($7,700)	($7,893)	($8,090)	($8,292)	($8,499)
Net worth at year end if property sold	$44,474	$48,301	$52,376	$56,722	$61,307

vacancy provision has been built in to allow for repair work as well as potential down-time when you cannot find a tenant.

The cash loss/gain is calculated from all financial transactions, including tax refunds. The profit figure does not include building depreciation because, in the vast majority of cases, this is clawed back by the IRD. The Internal Rate of Return (IRR) relates the profit made ($8174 in year 1) to the actual amount invested ($44,000). The equation is 8174 ÷ 44,000 x 100.

The gross value of the investment incorporates capital gains plus cash losses or gains (including tax refunds or payments), assuming you pay for losses as they are made and that any excess cash is reinvested. The net worth at year-end figure assumes that half of the chattels depreciation is clawed back by the IRD.

Key factors to consider in this example are the allowances made for unknown occurrences. If you have allowed for a vacancy rate then you won't lose sleep when your tenants inform you they are leaving. If you make adequate allowances for maintenance then you won't try and cut corners on repairs and end up with a poorly maintained property. Note the effects of selling costs on the rate of return. In the first year, selling costs reduce the return to 1.1%. However, by year five the average annual return is 7.8% and by year 10 it has increased to 10%. This clearly demonstrates why property is a long-term investment. Had the deposit been 10% rather 20% ($22,000 instead of $44,000), then the average annual IRR would be 13.1% after five years and 18.3% after 10 years.

Understanding the calculations involved in analysing your property investment is a complex area that investors commonly find quite difficult. We would strongly recommend you consult your accountant or someone who understands this area of property investment.

2

Goal Setting

Goal setting is important in most aspects of life and this is also true of property investment. Without a clear direction it is difficult to properly co-ordinate your efforts in establishing an investment that matches your lifestyle, financial and life situation, skills and aspirations.

✓ To begin with, ask yourself why you want to invest in property. What is the key reason? Is it to generate an income, is it to build wealth, is it a form of savings for retirement, or is it a combination of all these?

✓ Do you have an investment period in mind? For instance, you may want to retire in 20 years and provide a retirement income through property.

✓ What value of property do you want or need over this time period? To answer this you need to consider the income you want from property.

✓ What type of property will you purchase to meet your goal? Five two-bedroom flats or three three-bedroom houses, or something else?

You should write these goals down so that they are quantifiable within a time frame. (Remember that it's all about equity and cashflow, not necessarily the number of properties you own.)

Example

- I intend to retire in 15 years' time with a passive (no or minimal time input) annual income of $40,000 after tax in today's value.

- I will require a gross annual income from rents of $66,000 to allow for property management fees, repairs and maintenance, vacancies and tax.

- To achieve this income I intend to own six debt-free, two-bedroom units renting for $210 each per week.

Property investment strategy

You will need to establish a strategy for how you are going to achieve these goals and the rules you are going to follow. For instance:

✓ What are your requirements for choosing locations?

✓ What yield will you require?

✓ What minimum equity (10%, 20% 50%, etc.) will you maintain?

✓ How will you organise finance?

✓ What type of property will you purchase?

✓ What ownership structure will you use?

✓ Who will your target tenant market be?

You will need to determine how you will buy the properties, over what time period and how you will handle the debt. As an example, you could buy many growth properties and, at a predetermined point, sell some of them to pay off the remaining debt.

Alternatively, you could buy high-income producing property and pay off the mortgage.

Make sure your strategy is realistic and allows for risk factors such as mortgage rate increases or economic downturns. Remember that property is typically a long-term investment.

Example

- I intend to use the equity in my own home to buy a four-bedroom house near the university (with a section large enough to accommodate a second minor dwelling) for approximately $250,000 to produce a rental yield of at least 8%.

- In each bedroom I will install internet facilities and furnish with a bed and desk, increasing the achievable rent.

- I will construct a two-bedroom minor dwelling for $30,000, which will produce a rental yield of 34%.

- Once the project is completed, and producing a higher yield of around 11%, I will refinance for a fixed term of five years, paying interest only; this will allow me to buy more property.

- Using surplus rental income, I will purchase another similar property within one year and on average each subsequent year, until I have nine properties with a combined 33% equity.

- At a suitable period in time, I will sell six of the properties to own the remaining three properties mortgage free with a combined gross rental income of $90,000 per annum in today's dollars.

3

Structures for Owning Rental Property

When you are purchasing a rental property it is important to consider the most effective ownership structure for your particular set of circumstances. There are a number of different structures that may be used to own a rental property. It is imperative that you consult your accountant or lawyer on this matter in order to identify the best structure to achieve your property investment goals.

On most occasions, you will need to take into consideration estate planning and asset protection issues, which may or may not be compatible with advice that has been provided in relation to tax and income stream benefits.

For example, if you are involved in a separate business venture, you may wish to acquire investment properties by means of an independent entity, such as a family trust. Although this form of ownership would extend a level of protection against creditors of the business venture, there will be inherent tax disadvantages if the property operates at a loss. This is because the income tax legislation currently prevents losses being transferred out of a trust to the trustees and/or beneficiaries.

The following is a list of structures and their advantages and disadvantages.

1. Sole trader

ADVANTAGES	DISADVANTAGES
• simplicity: involves minimal set-up costs and administrative requirements • taxed at individual tax rates	• unlimited liability

2. Ordinary company

ADVANTAGES	DISADVANTAGES
• limited liability • taxed at the company tax rate of 33%	• increased level of administrative requirements

3. Loss attributing qualifying company (LAQC)

ADVANTAGES	DISADVANTAGES
• the company's losses are passed onto its shareholders, which may then be used to offset the shareholders' taxable income • dividends paid from capital gains are tax exempt in the hands of the shareholders	• shareholders are personally liable for the tax liabilities of the company

4. Partnership

ADVANTAGES	DISADVANTAGES
• easy to set up and low administration costs	• partners are jointly and severally liable for debts incurred in the partnership by the other partners

5. Trading trusts

ADVANTAGES	DISADVANTAGES
• provides opportunities for distributing income to beneficiaries	• property sold, gifted or transferred to a trust may trigger gift duty
• provides asset protection from creditors	• a trust is unable to distribute losses to beneficiaries

4

Taxation

When you own a rental property the Inland Revenue Department (IRD) treats you as a business. This means that you get the same tax deductions available to other businesses.

You can claim the costs involved in running your business, potentially including home office expenses, plus you can depreciate your business assets, including the rental property itself. This means that you pay tax on whatever is left over from your rental income less expenses and depreciation. Because you don't have to physically pay out depreciation in order for it to be a tax deduction, it is possible to structure your investment so that it is cashflow-positive but still make a tax loss. This tax loss then reduces other income tax you are required to pay, such as PAYE deductions. An example is given on page 33.

Expenses

As a rental property owner you are entitled to deduct certain expenses in running the rental property. This is known as 'revenue expenditure' and can include items such as:

✓ insurance

✓ property management

✓ repairs and maintenance

✓ interest on the mortgage

✓ land rates and water rates

✓ petrol used in carrying out property inspections

✓ legal costs in relation to obtaining finance

✓ a mobile phone, if you have sufficient property, so tenants can easily contact you

✓ home office expenses.

You will also incur expenditure in improving the property. This is known as 'capital expenditure' and is not tax deductible, but is usually depreciable. Some examples of capital expenditure include:

✓ extensions to the building, such as adding another room

✓ putting in a swimming pool

✓ buying a new stove or kitchen appliance

✓ putting in a new driveway

✓ building a carport or garage

✓ legal conveyancing costs

✓ carpets and curtains

✓ landscaping.

Claiming mortgage interest payments

As the mortgage is likely to be your largest expense, it is crucial that it is tax deductible. Which property the mortgage is secured

Example

Rental income	$15,000
Less expenses	
Mortgage interest	$11,000
Rates	$1000
Insurance	$300
Repairs	$750
Home office expenses	$500
Property manager fees	$1125
Total expenses	**$14,675**
Net profit	$325
Building depreciation	$2400
Chattels depreciation	$1500
	($3900)
Net loss	**($3575)**

against does not affect tax deductibility. To be a tax deductible expense, the mortgage must be used for the purpose of generating taxable income. In this regard, the mortgage must be used for purchasing the rental property that produces the rental income.

This may sound simple; however, many investors have got this wrong and found that their investment is not as profitable as they had hoped.

If you buy a rental property and raise 100% of the purchase price against the security of your own home and the rental property, then the mortgage interest is tax deductible. However, if you raise a mortgage to buy a new home and rent out your old home, then the mortgage is not tax deductible. This is because the purpose of the mortgage was to buy the new home, not the rental property.

If you are in any doubt whatsoever, consult a tax expert. If you do find yourself in the above situation, the problem can be sorted out through using different ownership structures, such as a loss attributing qualifying company.

Depreciation clawback

When you come to sell the rental properties, there may be an element of depreciation recovered. This arises when the sale price of the property exceeds the book value of the property. The depreciation recovered is the difference between the sale price or cost price (whichever is lower) and the book value. This difference is treated as taxable income to the vendor.

Any depreciation recovered is limited to the amount of depreciation that you have received. (See 'Valuation', pages 58–63, for minimising your exposure to paying depreciation clawback.)

Using the example at the top of the next page, if you sold the property for $190,000, then the depreciation recovered would be $190,000 minus $180,000 ($10,000).

If the property were sold for a lower amount than its adjusted book value, you cannot claim a deduction for the difference between the sale price and the adjusted book value.

If you stop renting a property – for example, to use it as your

Example

Initial cost of property	$200,000
Depreciation claimed over the years	($20,000)
Book value	$180,000
Property sold	$250,000
Depreciation recovered (200,000–180,000)	$20,000
Capital gain	$50,000
Tax payable ($20,000 x 33%, assuming a 33% tax rate)	$6600

own home — then at the start of the new tax year, you must make an adjustment as if you had sold it for its true market value.

Capital gains tax

In New Zealand there is not a complete capital gains tax; however, there is a partial one.

If you invest in property for the long term and your principal income is rental money, then there is no capital gains tax when you sell the property.

However, if you invest in property with the main aim of selling it for a profit, then your capital gains are taxable. This type of investor is primarily known as a property developer, as he or she is developing a property for sale, either by building it from scratch or enhancing it to a greater or lesser degree.

If you are a developer, *all* your property investments — even those that you have purchased primarily for rental income — will be taxed for capital gains if sold. Therefore, if you are an investor as well as developer, it is imperative that you separate the two activities completely. See a tax expert for advice.

Tax penalties

You should be aware that the IRD can impose significant penalties in cases where insufficient tax has been paid. Insufficient tax (also known as a tax shortfall) can arise in any number of situations. For instance, there may be a tax shortfall when a tax deduction for capital expenditure has been incorrectly claimed or where depreciation has been claimed at too high a rate.

In cases of tax shortfalls, penalties ranging from 20% to 150% of the shortfall may be imposed. The various types of penalties, in order, are as follows:

1. lack of reasonable care	20%
2. unacceptable interpretation	20%
3. gross carelessness	40%
4. abusive tax position	100%
5. tax evasion	150%

As a property investor, it is important that all your records are adequately maintained and kept up to date. This will ensure that the risk of having any of the above penalties applied to your investment is minimised. When you are unsure about a particular situation, always consult a professional in order to ensure you comply with the income tax legislation.

It is a good idea to follow up any verbal communication with the IRD with a letter, fax or email to confirm the conversation. Retain this paperwork for seven years, or as advised by your tax specialist, as you never know when you may need it.

Special tax codes

If you are going to make a tax loss on your rental property investment over the coming year, it is possible to access the tax savings on that loss before the end of the financial year. This opportunity is available only to salary and wage earners, who must complete the Inland Revenue form IR23B. After completion of the IR23B, the IRD will issue a certificate with a special tax code that you give your employer, who will then be entitled to deduct less PAYE from your wage or salary each pay period.

The advantages are that you receive your refund sooner and you achieve better cashflow.

The disadvantages are the potential to estimate the losses incorrectly, and the need to estimate your expected losses annually.

Financial information

There are many items that require consideration prior to and subsequent to rental property investment. Firstly, as outlined above, it is important that you have an appropriate ownership structure in place for your particular set of circumstances.

Time needs to be spent ensuring that all financial information required by the IRD and/or your accountant is accurately documented. This will help ensure that your rental statements are prepared correctly at the lowest cost and that all allowable deductions are maximised. Most accountants provide property investors with end-of-year checklists detailing the required information. This information is then used to produce the rental accounts.

The following procedures or techniques are advisable to ensure that your information is accurately maintained and used.

✓ Keep tenancy documentation separate from any accounting and tax documentation.

✓ Set up a separate bank account for your property investment activities only.

✓ Retain all invoices that are related to expenditure on rental investment activities, and keep in a separate file.

✓ If you have multiple properties, clearly identify income and expenditure for each separate property to ensure that you can analyse the performance of each property.

✓ Clearly identify the difference between capital injections and rental received.

✓ Keep a vehicle log book to identify when you have used your vehicle on rental property business.

Excellent computer software systems specifically designed for rental properties are available now. They can do more than just assist in the management of your financial transactions. See pages 137–139 for useful examples.

5

Finance

Financing a rental property is similar to financing your own home. These days, even the interest rate you pay for a residential rental property should be the same as your personal mortgage rate.

The key difference is that rental property finance, when correctly structured, is tax deductible. Because of this, any debt reduction you make should be concentrated on personal debt before rental property debt.

You can use equity in your home to ensure that your personal debt is minimised and eliminated as soon as possible. As an example, rather than using your own money as a deposit on a rental property, use it to pay off any personal debt. You can then use the equity in your own home as your security and obtain 100% finance for rental property.

As the equity in your rental properties increases, you can also use this as security for further rental property purchase, rather than using your own cash as deposit. Once again, your own cash can then be used to eliminate your personal debt.

Principal and interest vs interest only

Whether to pay principal plus interest (P&I) off your mortgage or interest only is a common question from many property investors. The answer depends on your personal circumstances.

Paying off principal and interest will save you money in the long term, is safer and eventually you will pay off the mortgage. However, there will be a negative influence on your cashflow situation, as extra money will be going towards your principal repayments. In addition, as you pay off your mortgage, the interest you can claim as a tax deduction will also reduce. This can lead you to paying tax on a book profit while you still have a negative cashflow.

If you are intending to acquire more rental properties, then you are probably better off with an interest-only mortgage: this will give you a better cashflow, which helps you borrow more money and buy more property. Your tax deduction on interest payments will continue because the size of your mortgage will not reduce.

If you still have a mortgage on your private home, again an interest-only mortgage on your rental property is the better option – use the surplus cashflow from the rental properties to pay off your personal, non tax-deductible mortgage.

Many investors cannot see how they can make money on their investment if they do not pay off the mortgage. The answer is that the equity is increasing as the value of the property increases. Through the positive effects of gearing, this capital growth usually increases your equity faster than you can by paying off the mortgage.

If you can purchase more properties through a better cashflow, then the benefits of leverage will usually give you a better return than a lower number of properties on P&I finance. The assumption here is that property values will grow. But if you own property in a low-growth area, then you would be better to buy a reduced number of properties and pay off the mortgages. This would be a strategy for a cautious investor.

Fixed or floating?

If timed right, fixed-term mortgages can save you a lot of money through lower interest rates over the fixed-rate period. The right time is when the average floating rate over the fixed-term period is higher than the fixed-term rate.

The problem is that interest rate variables are complex and very difficult to predict, even by experts. If you get it wrong, you could end up paying more with a fixed-term rate than you would on a floating rate.

Fixed-term rates are also inflexible. If you want to break them you have to pay a (tax-deductible) fee. So, if you had a sum of money that you wanted to use to reduce the principal, it would be more difficult with a fixed-term mortgage. Before entering a fixed-term mortgage, ensure you know what the cost of breaking the fixed term is, and how much principal you can repay, if any, without penalty fees.

However, fixed-term rates give you more certainty about the cost of what is likely to be your largest expense – your mortgage. This can make it easier for you to sleep at night, especially if your cashflow is tight and if a rise in interest rates means you would have to sell a property because you could no longer afford it.

Although variable-rate mortgages can adversely affect your cashflow, they can also provide flexibility by allowing you to pay off some principal without incurring penalties.

Rather than trying to pick what interest rates will do in the future, if you have more than one mortgage, it is usually a better idea to have some on floating rates and some on fixed.

As you buy more property and your loan balance increases, try and space out when the fixed-rate mortgages end so that you minimise the potential to have them all ending when interest rates are high. Unfortunately, this also means you would not have all your fixed-term loans ending when rates are unusually low.

Revolving credit

Revolving credit or lines of credit mortgages are another type of mortgage that can give you even more flexibility. These mortgages operate like an overdraft account. You have a limit on how much you can borrow, but you are only charged on the actual amount outstanding, calculated on a daily basis. You can make payments into the account at any time and can take money out of the account (up to the agreed limit) when you want to.

Although these types of loans used to have a higher interest rate than regular floating mortgages, currently many lenders are providing them at lower rates than regular floating mortgages. This may be because the banks know that having the facility sitting there waiting to be used is very tempting, and that people tend to borrow up to their limit and never actually pay the principal off.

If you have this type of facility you need to be disciplined. You must also avoid mixing non-deductible personal purchases in with investment debt, as this can lead to all sorts of problems.

How much can you borrow?

This is the big question and one you continually need to monitor if you want to build a portfolio of properties. You will need to know how each property purchase will affect your ability to borrow for any subsequent purchases.

How much you can borrow depends on your equity and

cashflow. Banks determine your equity with a formula called the Loan to Value Ratio or LVR, and your cashflow situation with the Debt Servicing Ratio or DSR.

Loan to Value Ratio (LVR)

The Loan to Value Ratio measures the security banks like to have should the investment go wrong and they have to sell the property to recover their money. They like to have a margin of 20% between the property's market value and the size of your loan, so that there is less chance of them losing their money. This 20% margin does not have to be in the rental property itself. They are happy to use your home as collateral.

Banks will actually lend 95% against property. However, they usually insist that you take out mortgage protection insurance to do this, and usually limit it to your own home. (You pay for the mortgage protection insurance, but it is the bank who receives all the benefit of the insurance.)

To calculate the LVR, simply divide the loan by the value of the property. For example, the LVR on a $100,000 property with a proposed $80,000 mortgage would be $80,000 \div $100,000 = 80\%$.

In this case the investment property could stand on its own without the need for other property as collateral. However, if the loan were higher or the property value lower, extra collateral would be required.

To work out your current borrowing limit, add up all your assets, deduct any outstanding loans, and multiply this by five. This is the total amount you could assume to borrow for purchasing investment property. If you take away the outstanding loan amount, this would be the value of rental property you could purchase with your current equity level.

Of course, there are many ways to buy better than market value, so you should not think you are in any way limited to this figure.

Example

Your home has a market value of $100,000 and a mortgage of $20,000. To work out the total value of rental property you could buy at market value, use the following calculation.

Own home, less mortgage $100,000 – $20,000 = $80,000

Equity times five $80,000 x 5 = $400,000

Potential borrowing,
  less home value $400,000 – $100,000 = $300,000

In this example, you could buy $300,000 of rental property, paying current market value, using the existing equity in your own home. This means you could buy three properties similar to your own before the bank would become nervous about your equity level.

Debt Servicing Ratio (DSR)

The Debt Servicing Ratio measures how easily you can afford the mortgage payments. The DSR is calculated in different ways by different lenders. However, the principle is the same: they merely apply different percentages. The equation is: loan payments divided by eligible income. As long as the result equals 1.0 or less, the bank should be happy with your serviceability.

Lenders generally allow 30% to 35% of your own income and 80% of your rental income to be eligible income applied to loan payments.

Example

You have an annual income of \$50,000, a home mortgage costing \$10,000 a year and you want to buy a rental property for \$100,000 — through 100% finance at 8% (\$8000 per year) — that is yielding 9% (\$9000) in rent.

- First, calculate the debt servicing:
  \$10,000 + \$8000 = \$18,000.

- Next, calculate your eligible income:
  \$50,000 x 30% + \$9000 x 80% (\$15,000 + \$7200) = \$22,500.

- The DSR would be \$18,000 ÷ \$22,500 = 0.8.

Balancing equity and cashflow

As a property investor, you need to balance equity and cashflow very carefully. Lenders require a positive outcome to both ratios, not just one. You may have all the equity in the world, but without sufficient cashflow it is unlikely you will be able to borrow. The same goes for high income but low equity or assets.

If your situation is balanced towards either assets or cashflow, this will affect the type of investment property you should be seeking.

If you have a high income but low level of assets, you should be looking at properties that are either a bargain or can have value added to them. By doing this you are addressing your potential weakness and strengthening yourself for future purchases.

Likewise, if you have a high net worth but low income, seek rental properties that provide high rental yields.

By ensuring that you are purchasing property that either helps your potential weakness or maintains your equity/cashflow balance, you will place yourself in a better position to be able to borrow to fund more rental properties in the future.

Applying for finance

When applying for finance, go fully prepared with all the necessary documentation. This includes: proof of income; three months' bank statements to show how you handle money; proof of assets; a finance statement of assets and liabilities; and a cashflow projection for the property.

Banks make money by lending money, so approach them as if you were presenting them with a good business opportunity. Banks are affected by how they perceive your character and your presentation. Wear smart clothes and always be professional in all your dealings with them.

A cost-free alternative is to use the services of a mortgage broker.

Using a mortgage broker

An ideal way to check out the mortgage market to ensure you are getting the right type of loan and combination of good conditions, lowest fees and interest rate is to use a mortgage broker. Best of all their service is free — music to the ears of all property investors.

Mortgage brokers should be able to save you time and give good and unbiased advice. To ensure you are dealing with a reputable broker, make sure he or she is a member of the New Zealand Mortgage Brokers Association. Members are held accountable to the association and cannot contravene the association's code of ethics. Seek a broker who is experienced, not just with finance but with investment property as well.

Finance tips

✓ Internet or phone banking facilities make it very easy to keep up to date with rental payments.

✓ As you buy more property, don't have all your borrowings with one bank.

✓ Always negotiate fees. Property investors make good clients for banks – make sure they appreciate your business.

✓ Ensure that your borrowing is structured to buy investment property so that mortgage interest is tax deductible.

✓ Don't pay principal and interest when you still have private debt that is not tax deductible.

✓ Don't pay principal and interest when you are actively buying rental property.

✓ Mix your debt between floating and fixed-rate mortgages.

✓ Structure fixed-rate mortgages to end at different times to reduce the risk of them all falling due when rates are high.

✓ Don't mix private expenditure with a revolving credit facility.

✓ Have separate bank accounts for your rental properties and personal requirements.

6

Legal Issues

The role of the lawyer in property investment

The lawyer often acts as the co-ordinator or project manager and liaises with other professional advisors. His or her initial job is to undertake enquiries in relation to title, town planning matters, and so on. In consultation with accountants, your lawyer can provide information on the most advantageous purchasing structure and identify the options available to you.

Your lawyer should review the Agreement for Sale and Purchase prior to signing (this will allow him or her the opportunity to draft special conditions of sale) and all legal documentation associated with purchase, including the Land Information Memorandum (LIM) report, terms and conditions of loan approval, and any documentation necessary to create the purchasing entity (such as LAQC, family trust or trading trust).

It is best for your lawyer to handle all the paperwork such as preparation of security documentation for the mortgage lender, co-ordination of settlement, including draw-down of loan advance, registration of securities and checking that water rates and land rates for the property are cleared on settlement.

In addition, your lawyer should identify and discuss issues associated with the purchase, such as de facto relationship issues, updating wills, and so on.

There are myriad legal acts that may affect you. These include the Residential Tenancies Act, Privacy Act, Fair Trading Act, Consumer Guarantees Act, Fencing Act, Resource Management Act and Building Act. Although you should have a good working knowledge of the Residential Tenancies Act, your lawyer should advise you on relevant legislation that could affect you or your investment.

Your responsibilities when purchasing

Determine the essential components of your own responsibilities in acquiring investment properties.

✓ Nominate the entity that will complete the purchase.

✓ Organise the loan.

✓ Arrange insurance for the dwelling and, where relevant, any contents.

✓ Organise the transfer of utilities (gas, power and telephone).

✓ Sign the bond transfer forms where relevant.

✓ Contact existing tenants with details of manner by which rental is to be paid.

Land Information Memorandum (LIM)

The law requires the local district or city council to issue a report called a Land Information Memorandum (LIM) about a specific property upon request by any person. The LIM contains a range of information about the property.

To request a LIM contact the appropriate council and complete a LIM request form. You will be required to pay the fee at this point. The cost varies depending on the council, but is generally between $250 and $300 including GST. Regulations state that the LIM must be issued within 10 working days from the date of the request. Most LIMs are issued between five and nine working days from the date of the request.

A LIM is prepared for the purposes of section 44A of the Local Government Official Information & Meetings Act 1987 and not for any other purpose. This means it is not designed to provide you with all the information you may need before making a property purchase.

A LIM does not usually include information that is available directly from the District Plan. The information provided in a LIM is based on a search of the council's database records and not an inspection of the property. Accordingly, the LIM does not necessarily reflect the current status of a property. Some examples of situations that affect the property but are not recorded in the LIM include: unauthorised works not known to the council, and breaches of consents or licences that are not the subject of a formal requisition or notice.

The information in a LIM

A LIM contains a range of information relevant to a particular property. This includes:

✓ details of the current annual land and water rates and balance owing

✓ information about special features or characteristics of the land that is known to the council but not included in the District Plan

✓ private and public stormwater and sewerage drainage plans as shown in the council's records

✓ information concerning any consent, certificate (including certificates issued by a building certifier), notice or order affecting the land or any building on the land previously issued by the council. This relates to building consents, resource consents, liquor licences, registration of food premises, dangerous goods licences, building warrants of fitness, compliance schedules, code compliance certificates, etc.

✓ outstanding requisitions or notices being written notification from the council informing the owner and/or occupier of the property that certain aspects of that property do not meet council specifications and require remedial action

✓ information relating to the use to which that land may be put and conditions attached to that use

✓ information that has been notified to the council by any statutory organisation having the power to classify land or buildings for any purpose (e.g. Department of Conservation, the Historic Places Trust)

✓ information that has been notified to the council by any network utility operator (e.g. United Power, Watercare Services, Enerco Gas) under the Building Act 1991

✓ other information concerning the property, that the council may also see fit to add.

Property file search

A property file is a council's physical file record of the building consents/permits held in respect of the property specified. It contains a limited amount of information relevant to a particular property. It may include: files of applications for building consents/permits, associated plans and documents and amended plans. Some plans for the property may be on microfiche and will be made available to view. The search of the property file does not include a search of council's computer databases or other physical files. A property file is not a substitute for a Land Information Memorandum.

To conduct a property file search, you need to make a request in writing on the 'Request to View Property File' form available from the local council. Alternatively, you can make a phone request and complete the form when you go to view the file. The property file will be available to view approximately one full working day after your request.

The limitations of the property file

Because the information available in a property file is limited to the council's physical file only, it does not reflect the current status of a property. Examples of information that affect the property but are not evident in the property file include:

✓ unauthorised works not known to the council and/or breaches or consents or licences that are not the subject of a formal requisition or notice

✓ District Plan information

✓ requisitions

✓ hazards

✓ details of contaminated sites

✓ licensing of premise details or warrant of fitness compliance

✓ pool fencing compliance.

Some information covered by the Privacy Act 1993 and/or the Local Government & Meetings Act 1987 could be withheld from the property file.

Common legal mistakes to be avoided

✓ Failing to document representations that have been made by a vendor within the Agreement for Sale and Purchase.

✓ Choosing the wrong entity to complete the purchase.

✓ Failing to identify and/or address conditions imposed by the lender in approving finance application.

✓ Lack of organisation, resulting in an inability to meet conditional dates and deadlines.

✓ Using information obtained on a prior transaction that is not relevant to a current transaction.

✓ Failing to appoint advisors who are experienced with the specific issues that arise in property investment.

Legal checklists

Prior to presentation of offer

☐ Obtain a copy of the Certificate of Title.

❏ Obtain a copy of a LIM report if possible. (In some circumstances, you may find that a vendor has a copy of a recent LIM report. Where the property is to be purchased through a real estate agent, you may discover that a prior unsuccessful purchaser has obtained a LIM report, and is prepared to transfer the same to you at a fraction of the standard cost.)

❏ Search the property file at the relevant council offices.

❏ Determination of associated issues and contacting relevant bodies — for example, Transit New Zealand, in circumstances where there is potential for roading changes to impact upon the area in which you are purchasing.

❏ Obtain copies of all relevant tenancy agreements.

❏ Obtain pre-approved funding, and in particular, address any special conditions that may be imposed by the lender.

❏ Determine the costs of professional charges, body corporate fees, contributions to land rates, etc.

❏ Obtain a copy of the body corporate rules, if applicable.

❏ Identify any special conditions or warranties that you want to have included in the Agreement for Sale and Purchase — such as that the current owner will remove all rubbish and debris from the property, fix a broken window or have the carpets cleaned. (These clauses, which will need to be drafted by a professional, should allow you to retain funds on settlement if the vendor fails to comply.)

Presentation of offer

☐ Identify the entity that will purchase the property (e.g. private individual, partnership, limited liability company, LAQC or family trust).

☐ If you are uncertain what entity will have ownership of the property, add the words 'or nominee' immediately following the legal description of the purchaser.

☐ Carefully consider the two most important aspects of the transaction: the purchase price and the settlement date. Often the purchaser focuses solely on the purchase price and fails to appreciate that this is inherently linked to the settlement date. An early settlement date may result in the vendor accepting a lower purchase price.

☐ How will you pay the deposit? It is preferable to pay a minimal deposit on signing the agreement, with any balance to be paid only upon the agreement being rendered unconditional in all respects. It is wise not to pay the deposit until your lawyer has had the opportunity of looking over the agreement.

☐ Identify and record all relevant tenancies that will remain in place following settlement.

☐ Identify and record all chattels for which the ownership is to pass to the purchaser on settlement.

☐ Insert a condition rendering the agreement conditional upon the receipt of a satisfactory LIM.

☐ Insert a clause specifying the time frame by which the

vendor must accept the offer. This provides an incentive for the vendor to accept it and not wait for better offers.

❑ A large number of conditions within the Agreement for Sale and Purchase may be viewed negatively by the vendor. In this case, insert a single due diligence condition (as opposed to a solicitor's approval clause) in the following format:

This agreement is conditional upon the purchaser satisfying himself/herself that the property is suitable for his/her purpose in all respects, and in particular, without affecting the generality of the afore-said, the purchaser is entitled to take into consideration the commercial aspects of the transaction.

The decision of the purchaser shall be final and absolute, and the vendor shall not be entitled to enquire into the reasons for the purchaser's decision hereunder.

This condition is to be satisfied within five working days from the date of this agreement, and in the event that the purchaser shall give notice of non-satisfaction of this condition, then this agreement shall be deemed void and the deposit shall forthwith be refunded to the purchaser in full and neither party shall have any claim as against the other whatsoever.

Following acceptance of the offer by the vendor

❑ Arrange appointment with all relevant advisors to ensure co-ordination of settlement.

❑ Appoint a project manager (usually your solicitor) to oversee the settlement process, timetable compliance dates (e.g. processing of loan documentation), and so on.

❑ Personally diarise any conditional dates.

❑ Follow up with lender with particular reference to compliance with any special conditions of loan offer (e.g. obtaining valuations).

❑ Where the property is tenanted, try and meet with the tenant/s.

Once the agreement is unconditional

❑ Arrange insurance cover, and forward details to your solicitor. Note that each lender has their own requirements, details of which will have been sent to your solicitors.

❑ Determine location of keys for all external doors and details of any burglar alarm code.

❑ Where there are recently acquired chattels (e.g. whiteware), ascertain whether there are guarantees/warranties, and arrange for these to be made available to you on settlement.

❑ Arrange a pre-settlement inspection. (This can be difficult in properties that are tenanted.)

❑ Obtain from your solicitor a statement of funds to be received and dispersed on settlement, including details of your solicitor's account.

❑ Where there is a shortfall between the purchase price and the amount to be borrowed, arrange for sufficient funds to be available to your solicitor on or before settlement date.

7

Valuations to Maximise Depreciation

It is important to document the value of your investment property. Once you have bought the right property in the right location and made the planned improvements, you can get new valuations: a property valuation and a chattels valuation.

The property valuation is to show the bank that you can increase the size of the mortgage and get your deposit back, or that you have increased the value of your portfolio and can use the equity for more property purchases.

The chattels valuation is to make your depreciation claim as large and accurate as possible. Chattels wear out faster than the main structure of the building and therefore need to be replaced more often. Hence the IRD allows you to depreciate chattels at a higher rate, which maximises your tax deduction.

Property valuations

A property valuation is to provide an expert opinion on the market value of a property.

Market value is an objective estimate of what a party is likely to pay for an asset on any given day. It is defined by the New Zealand Property Institute (NZPI) as 'the estimated amount for which an asset should exchange on the date of valuation betwee a willing buyer and a willing seller in an arm's-length transaction after proper marketing wherein the parties had each acted knowledgeably, prudently, and without compulsion'.

The Valuer Act 1948 provides protection to the public by preventing unqualified persons from acting as valuers of land (real property). Under this legislation, parties are required to meet certain requirements, be of good character and comply with rigorous standards to become a registered public valuer (registered valuer). The act also provides recourse for members of the public in the event of a registered valuer acting in a negligent manner.

To be a registered valuer and obtain an annual practising certificate, the professional must also be a member of the NZPI. This institute provides a framework for continuing education and ensuring high levels of competency. The NZPI, which was formed in January 1999, has combined the services of property valuers, plant and equipment valuers, property managers and property consultants to create a unified property profession.

General report content

As a minimum, a property report should include the following:

- ✓ address of property, description of locality, description of land, description of improvements (buildings), zoning and legal description
- ✓ comment on Certificate of Title (copy should be provided) and anything recorded upon it
- ✓ basis of valuation
- ✓ market commentary

'usion

ble sales (minimum of four)

recommendation (if for lending purposes)

✓ state that the valuer is a registered public valuer under the Valuers Act 1948

✓ state that the valuer holds professional indemnity insurance

✓ state that the report has been prepared in accordance with NZPI valuation standards.

Fees and timing

Fixed fees should be agreed in advance if possible — a valuer will often request details about the property to assess the size of the job. Disbursements are sometimes included in the fee estimate; however, it is prudent to check so there are no surprises. If disbursements are additional, check whether they are to be charged at cost. Some firms may add a premium on top to cover operating expenses.

Chattel valuations

It is possible to comply with IRD requirements and depreciate components of your rental property at up to 60% of DV (or Diminishing Value), as opposed to 4% for buildings. Many property investors and property professionals are often unaware that this level of depreciation can be claimed.

A specialised chattels and fit-out apportionment completed on investment properties not only maximises cashflow for the investor, but also reduces clawback tax when you sell the property.

In 1993 the IRD revised the depreciation schedule and the current schedule allows greater scope for property investors.

The three main benefits of having a specialised apportionment are: maximising depreciation, minimising depreciation recovery and reduced risk of penalties.

By splitting the purchase price of your investment property into the various depreciation categories set by IRD, you will increase your depreciation claim. Many investors claim nominal depreciation based on the value of chattels assessed by a registered valuer. However, this value is assessed for finance purposes, and will not maximise the depreciation claimable by property investors.

The three main categories that should be included in an apportionment report for depreciation are:

✓ land: non depreciable

✓ building fit-out & chattels: depreciable at 7.5%–60%

✓ building structure: depreciable at 4% DV.

Chattels is the first category for depreciation of residential rental properties. This includes assets such as: carpets, blinds, stove and light fittings.

Building fit-out is the second category for depreciation of residential rental properties. This includes assets such as: electrical reticulation, plumbing fixtures, fences and partitions (non-load bearing).

These assets are a small sample of the various assets that can be separated from the building structure for depreciation purposes. By apportioning the correct depreciation rates as specified by IRD you can maximise your depreciation claim and therefore maximise your cashflow.

Example 1 — New dwelling

Depreciation without apportionment	year 1	$7800
Depreciation with apportionment	year 1	$15,000
Additional depreciation	year 1	$7200

Example 2 — Older dwelling

Depreciation without apportionment	year 1	$4200
Depreciation with apportionment	year 1	$6500
Additional depreciation	year 1	$2300

Minimise depreciation recovery

Some investors do not claim depreciation on their rental property due to the possibility of depreciation recovery. A specialised depreciation apportionment can benefit you when you sell the property, however. By having the apportionment completed upon purchase of the property you will be provided with a full breakdown of the individual assets such as carpets and curtains.

It is very rare that many of the assets shown in the apportionment would increase in value over the time of ownership.

The depreciation on these assets is therefore allowed and recovery is reduced.

Example — Carpets

Purchase price (apportioned)	$4000
Depreciation claimed	($3000)
Written-down value	$1000

It is hard to prove that the carpets have increased in value. In reality, the written-down value of $1000 will be a true indication of their value.

8

Risk Analysis

Successful business people consider their risks in business and then put in place mechanisms to minimise those risks. The same principles apply to being in the business of property investing. Consider your risk profile, as a property investor, and consider which risks you are prepared to accept and how to minimise or eliminate other risks.

You should periodically consider your risk profile as it will change over time as your circumstances change.

Property investment can be a very exciting or a very stressful activity. When values and rents are decreasing it is comforting to know you have reduced risk because you clearly identified your risks of investing and took steps to minimise those risks. The following information is to highlight some of the risks you may not currently appreciate or be protecting yourself against.

Risks of overborrowing

Fixed-rate mortgages help property investors manage debt, but you should always allow for higher interest rate payments.

If your cashflow situation is so poor that a 1% or 2% interest rate increase would force you to sell the property, then think carefully before committing to it. (This area is covered further in 'Finance', see pages 39–47.)

When considering a property purchase, do an interest rate risk analysis. As an example, the extra cost of a two percentage points rise in interest rates (say from 7% to 9%) on a $200,000 mortgage is $4000 a year. Could you absorb this cost or would you be forced to sell?

Interest rate changes

As previously mentioned, mortgage payments are usually your largest expense and increasing interest rates are a large risk. If you have over borrowed, then you risk losing your entire investment. However, if you have not structured your finance correctly you risk reducing your return.

Fixed-rate mortgages offer insurance against interest rate rises, as does careful finance planning.

Fall in tenant demand

Your best strategy against low tenant demand is to buy a property that suits a large number of potential tenants and is well maintained.

At times of falling demand, the rental prices of poorly presented and poorly maintained properties fall first and fall hardest. Always ensure that your property is well maintained and presented, and know the largest tenant group in the area and what types of property and features they most want.

If you know that market rental prices have fallen, don't be too slow in reducing your rental prices. It is better to lower your price by $10 a week and get a tenant quickly than hold out for the higher rent. By holding out for a higher rent, you risk getting a poor tenant that other landlords don't want and it may take six months to recoup the loss of just one week's rent.

When a tenant gives notice ask why he or she is leaving and see if there is anything you can do to change the decision.

Low or negative capital growth

The property market can go up and down and you need to be prepared for this. If you have owned the property for only a few years, then you may need to ride out the downturn.

Make sure when you purchase a rental property that you are buying in an area that has a better than average potential to increase in value, over the next few years at least. Consider factors such as economics, lifestyle and demographics on which to base your decision.

Be aware of what level of negative growth the bank would become uneasy about your equity situation.

Damage to property

Your best defence against property damage is good tenant selection and active property management. Most tenants are good at keeping the property well looked after; however, it pays to check up on them to ensure that they do.

Keeping the property well maintained shows you care about it and this attitude often rubs off on the tenants. Regular inspections keep you abreast of any damage. Do not confuse damage with fair wear and tear. If damage does occur, get on to it quickly and discuss it with your tenants. Offer them the opportunity to arrange for it to be fixed and state the quality level that you expect.

If you have a disagreement with the tenants, see 'When Things Go Wrong With a Tenancy', pages 112–125.

Some insurance policies cover damage to property, so you can pay to pass on the risk.

Tenant failing to pay rent

As with damage to your property, your best defence is good tenant selection and active property management. Keep a close eye on rent payments — if they are missed, immediately issue a 10-day notice. (See 'When Things Go Wrong With a Tenancy', pages 112–125.)

Demographic changes

Are there demographic changes occurring? Consider such factors as the ageing population, population movements (south/north drift) and changing lifestyle considerations. These can all have an effect on your investment over time. When planning your investment strategy, it is good to consider these changes and the effect they will have in 10, 20 or even 30 years' time.

New legislation

New legislation is being introduced into Parliament all the time, some of it 'good' and some of it 'bad' for property investors. Often politicians and their advisors have little idea of how the property investment market works, and changes may have different effects than anticipated. The income-related rents scheme, reintroduced by the Labour government in December 2000 to force private sector rents down, is a perfect case. As state rents became artificially cheap, the number of occupants per dwelling fell. This increased demand for private accommodation, which helped increase private rental prices.

Read newspapers and magazines to keep up-to-date with these changes, and join your local property investors association. Part of your membership fee goes towards the NZPIF, which keeps a close eye on Parliament and lobbies on your behalf.

Loss of primary income

If you lost your primary source of income, how would this affect your property investments? If the potential consequences are high, you may like to consider income protection insurance.

Mortality

How would your dependents cope financially if you were to die unexpectedly? Would they be able to keep any or all of the rental properties? Would this investment provide sufficient income for them to cope financially? Would they need to have the mortgage paid off or extra funds? See 'Insurance', pages 74–81, to work out how much life insurance you need.

9

Checklist for Deciding on a Property

Below are some handy hints that you could use as checklists when buying a property. You want to make sure that you have done a thorough check of the issues that may affect your ownership of the property, issues relating to upgrading the property, ongoing maintenance, and the ability to let the property and get good rentals through appealing to tenants.

The location

☐ What is the zoning? Is it residential?

☐ Does the area have the amenities you need — shops, schools, transport, etc?

☐ Is the electricity, sewer connected?

☐ Are there any major developments going on in the area in the future — proposed motorway, new shops, etc?

Land

☐ Is it free from filling, excess seepage of water, steep grading, dense trees, loose boulders, etc? If you are considering extensions, an engineer's report may be necessary to access the land.

❏ Is it free from landslips? Check with your local council and if necessary obtain a geo-technical engineer's report.

❏ Check the lawns for puddles as these can indicate poor drainage.

Building

❏ Is the paintwork in good condition?

❏ Are the internal and external walls free from cracks?

❏ Are the roofing, guttering and downpipes in good condition?

❏ Is the building free from damp? Signs of damp, especially rising damp, are usually found around window sills, chimney-breasts, in ceilings and under floor coverings.

❏ Is the floor level and in sound condition? Using a marble is a good test for level floors.

❏ Is the plaster in good condition?

❏ What sort of insulation do the walls and ceilings have?

❏ Does the house have good ventilation and natural lighting?

❏ Turn on all the taps and check for water pressure, and that water drains away quickly.

❏ Turn on the lights to see if they are working. If they are not working, it may be just replacing the bulb or a more serious electrical problem.

❏ Check number of power points and if they are suitably located.

❏ Establish exactly what is included in the price of the house – carpets, drapes, appliances, light fittings, etc.?

❏ Check that any appliances included are working: stove, air conditioning, heaters, bathroom fans. If it has a fireplace, ask when it last had the chimney swept.

❏ Does the house have good storage?

❏ Will the house be expensive to maintain?

❏ Are doorways and passageways wide enough to move furniture through?

Bedrooms

❏ Will the bedrooms be affected by light and noise – are they close to a street, to street lamps, etc.?

❏ Are the bedrooms located so they are reasonably free from living area noise? This is often important in flatting situations.

❏ Is there sufficient ventilation?

❏ Is there a wardrobe or storage space? Will bedroom furniture fit?

Bathroom and toilet

❏ Is there sufficient ventilation?

❏ Is there an extractor fan to remove steam?

☐ Is the shower recess or bathtub free from leaks and sealed soundly?

☐ Is there a power point?

☐ Are there towel rails, cupboards, mirror?

☐ Is the toilet in good condition and does it flush properly?

Kitchen

☐ Are there sufficient cupboards for storage, and adequate bench space for preparing and serving food?

☐ Do the cupboards open and shut properly and is there room to add more?

☐ What is the condition of the stove? Is there an exhaust fan? Try the elements to see if they work.

☐ Will a regular-size refrigerator, dishwasher and/or microwave fit?

☐ Is there sufficient lighting and ventilation?

Dining and living rooms

☐ Will the furniture fit?

☐ Is there room for an extended dining room table?

☐ Are there sufficient power points?

☐ Is there heating? What type — gas, electric — and is it expensive to run?

☐ Does it have a TV aerial?

Laundry

☐ Does it have a laundry tub?

☐ Is the hot water connected?

☐ Could a standard washing machine be installed without any problems?

☐ Is there room for a dryer?

☐ Does it have any cupboards or storage?

☐ Is there a floor waste (drain) or is the floor sufficiently graded so any overflow of waste can escape without causing damage?

Outside area

☐ Are the paths and fences in good condition?

☐ Is there a garage or carport? If not, can one be put on?

☐ How much maintenance does the garden require? Tenants don't tend to be good gardeners.

☐ Are the lawns easy to mow?

☐ Can the grounds be improved? Landscaping can be a cost-effective way to add value.

☐ Is there a pool? If so, does it comply with safety standard regulations?

☐ Is there plenty of parking? Is there space to lay pavers to park on?

10

Insurance

Property insurance

Before finalising the purchase of your rental property, you will
need to arrange adequate insurance cover.

There are a number of options available for this type of cover,
with some policies providing wider cover than others. Most
insurance companies will provide insurance cover on a tenanted
property at similar rates to that of an owner-occupied property. It
is important to tell the insurer that the property is going to be
rented, as failure to do so could result in a declined claim.

A standard dwelling policy for a rental property will insure the
property on a 'defined events' basis. This means that in the event
of damage occurring to the property, you will only be able to have
a claim met if the damage was a result of one of the events set out
in the policy. The normal events that you claim for with this type
of cover are: fire, explosion and lightning; storm or flood; water
damage from any domestic water system on or around the house;
impact damage by a vehicle or animal; and breakage of fixed glass
or sanitaryware forming part of the house.

The amount that you can claim with this type of policy is
limited to the indemnity value (that is, the market value less the
value of the land), with a maximum dollar value in the event of a
total loss.

Standard dwelling policies exclude certain events when the house is tenanted. This means that you would not be able to claim for damage caused to the property by the tenants or by anybody they allow onto the property. Some insurance companies will cover your rental property for malicious damage if you specifically request it. There will be a small increase in premium for this, and often there is a condition of having regular inspections of the property.

You would also be unable to claim for water damage that occurs over a period of time. This is called gradual deterioration and is excluded on all policies except owner-occupied dwellings.

Consider cover for chattels such as carpets, blinds, drapes, light fittings and appliances (the stove, provided it is permanently wired, is considered part of the structure). Some policies have a nominal cover for chattels in the dwelling policy.

There are now at least two policies that are specially designed for property investors. These protect against the tenant leaving when owing rent or being evicted for non-payment of rent. They also include cover for malicious damage and chattels. The annual premium for this cover is normally based on the amount of rent you receive and would cost about one week's rent plus GST per annum. The rental property policies may be restricted to investors who have their properties professionally managed.

When deciding on the type of policy you want for your rental property, remember that the cheapest insurance usually provides the lowest cover.

Personal insurance

The goal of investing in property is often to provide financial independence or an income for retirement, and investors generally have a high level of borrowings to achieve their goals. There is always the risk that some unforeseen event could inhibit your plans to achieve your goals.

The basis of insurance is that the insured passes the cost of adverse events that he or she is unable to fund, or is not prepared to fund, should the event occur.

The decision as to how far you go towards protecting yourself from risk is an individual choice. However, many property investors never consider the risks they face or the consequences of those risks. This can be a severe mistake. There are four areas of risk which should be assessed on a regular basis: serious illness, serious hospitalisation, inability to earn an income, and death. The following are insurance products that can protect you financially from these four areas of risk:

✓ *Serious illness – living assurance:*
   This provides a lump sum to help you reduce debts if you suffer a trauma or critical illness.

✓ *Serious hospitalisation – health insurance:*
   This covers costs for major medical expenses as a result of either an illness or injury. This also provides you with immediate treatment by using the private health system.

✓ *Unable to earn an income – disability income (income protection insurance):*
   This is to ensure you retain an income and are able to maintain your lifestyle in the event of an illness or injury keeping you off work.

✓ *Total and permanent disablement:*
   This provides you with a lump sum if you are unable to ever work again.

✓ *Death – life cover:*
  This is to eliminate debts and provide replacement income for
  dependants in the event of an untimely death.

The purpose of an insurance plan is to cover the eventualities that
could, in a worst-case scenario, cause you to be in a worse position
than when you started your investment plan. It is important to
remember that every investor's situation will be different, and you
should plan accordingly.

These are some of the risks that need to be considered when
looking at an insurance plan for yourself or your family. None of us
like insurance but it is an important part of our wealth-creation
strategies. We are all comfortable insuring our property, but when
it comes to insuring ourselves we are more reluctant. Which is the
most important to you?

Use the chart on pages 80–81 to help you work out your own
life insurance requirements. The example is based on a number of
assumptions. You may decide you don't need an education fund, or
that the monthly payments in this example are too high or low. In
the example on page 78, Joe and Mary have decided, if one of
them died, to be in a better financial position than they are now,
but you may simply want to maintain your financial situation. It is
up to you to decide what is relevant for your personal situation.
Increasing your life cover may not cost a lot each month, so check
the numbers before making your final decision.

The amount of life cover you need should reduce every year as
your assets increase and debt decreases. Review it annually to
make sure that you have the right amount of cover to meet your
changing requirements.

Example

Mary and Joe started investing five years ago and have six investment properties in their portfolio. The purpose of their property investment is to provide financial freedom for the family, and thus allow them a better lifestyle, an early retirement and an above-average retirement income. Joe works and earns a gross income of $70,000 per annum and Mary looks after their two children. Some of the household income is spent paying the shortfall of property expenses not covered by the rent alone. Consider the following situations:

- Joe becomes disabled through sickness or an accident and is unable to work for 12 months. ACC would pay 80% of Joe's income (up to a maximum of $1465 per week, at the time of publication of this book) if his disability was caused by an accident, but not if it was due to illness (75% of cases).

- Joe is totally disabled (financially dead) and is unable to ever return to the workforce. Could Mary go out to work and earn a similar income and become the financial provider for the family? Who would look after the children?

- Joe died suddenly. How would Mary pay the living costs and continue to pay the extra expenses on their rental properties? Would she have to go back into the workforce? Can she earn a similar income? Who would look after the children?

- Mary died suddenly or has an accident or illness that meant she could not look after the children. Would Joe have to pay for full-time childcare? Could he afford this and the debt repayments?

An income protection tip

With income protection cover, there is usually a choice of four, eight or 13-week stand-down periods — that is, the length of time before you receive a benefit. If you have a reserve fund — which should be equivalent to three months' expenditure — then you can reduce the stand-down period on your income policy. This reserve could be within a revolving credit facility on your mortgage or set aside in a high-interest cash account. Changing from four to 13 weeks you can cut your annual premiums by 40% to 50%. That's a big saving annually! If you have a sick leave entitlement, this should make up part of your emergency fund.

Notes to the chart on pages 80 and 81

$150,000 is to pay off the existing personal mortgage. Joe's current net income per month is approximately $4000. The $3000 income figure for Mary was used because the $150,000 mortgage was paid off, therefore Mary needs less income per month to live; $2000 was used for Joe, if Mary died, because he could keep working and the $2000 per month would cover full-time childcare. Joe has a work-subsidised superannuation scheme currently worth $50,000. The total capital figures do require some analysis, so work with an insurance specialist to identify your individual requirements.

How to calculate the amount of life cover you need

Calculating insurance cover needs on the death of

	Joe	Mary
CASH NEEDS (to pay immediate expenses)		
Final expenses (funeral, legal, medical)	$10,000	$10,000
Administration costs	$0	$0
Repay mortgages, hire purchase, etc.	$150,000	$150,000
Education fund	$100,000	$100,000
Other cash needs	$0	$0
Total cash needs	$260,000	$260,000
INCOME NEEDS (to provide income for dependants)		
What after-tax income would you like your dependants to receive in the event of your death (monthly)?	$3000	$2000

	20 years	20 years
How many years do you wish to provide this?		
Investment earning rate (after tax) %	5	5
Capital required to meet income needs	$460,700	$307,133
Total capital required to meet income needs	$720,700	$567,133
LESS FUNDS AVAILABLE		
Existing life insurances	$0	$0
Superannuation benefits	$50,000	$0
Saleable asset	$0	$0
Other available funds	$0	$0
Total funds available	$50,000	$0
LIFE COVER NEEDS (shortfall)	**$670,700**	**$567,133**

11

Subdivision

The subdivision of land or buildings can add significant value to an investment.

The subdivision and sale of a section from a residential investment property can increase equity in the investment or provide a deposit for the next investment without affecting rental returns on the existing property. Subdivision of the separate tenancies within a building can provide the owner with increased liquidity (allowing the sale of smaller investment units) and will generally significantly increase the total value of the investment.

Subdivision of land and buildings is governed by a variety of legislation and local authority rules. It is important that a thorough investigation of local authority and other requirements is undertaken prior to making any investment decision that is dependent on completing a subdivision. Keep in mind that the subdivision process can take months to complete.

The subdivision process

Step 1: investigation and application
Before beginning the subdivision process, consult with the local council's planning staff about District Plan rules that may apply, and ascertain the type of application that will be required.

The next step is to employ a representative, usually a registered surveyor, who will advise on how to subdivide your property and draw up a proposed subdivision (scheme plan). This plan and accompanying report are submitted to the council for subdivision consent, a process that takes approximately 20 working days to complete. After initial assessment, you may be asked to provide further information such as geo-technical reports or flood-plan assessments.

The council will determine whether the application needs to be publicly notified — giving the public an opportunity to make submissions on the proposed subdivision. If submissions are made, the council will hold a hearing before deciding whether or not to grant the application.

As well as subdivision consent, you may need to apply for land use consent. This is required for things like vegetation removal and earthworks, and if proposed sites are too small to meet density requirements.

Step 2: subdivision consent
A subdivision consent is valid for two years. It is granted subject to certain conditions, which may include the following:

✓ *Reserves contribution:*
  All subdivisions involving the creation of a new lot will incur
  a reserves contribution. This is based on 6% (plus GST) of any
  new lot's value. You will be required to pay the cost of the
  council obtaining this valuation. On larger subdivisions
  the contribution could be land (of similar value) or money.
  Although the applicant can offer either, the final decision
  is at the council's discretion.

✓ *Other financial contributions:*
The creation of new sites can impact on existing council services in the area, which may then need to be upgraded to meet increased demand. Financial contributions for upgrading water supply, sewerage, storm-water treatment and disposal, and roading may be required. The monetary value of upgrading most areas has already been assessed. To find out what applies, contact the council prior to lodging your application. This will assist you to cost out the proposed subdivision.

✓ *Engineering conditions:*
To service the site you may need to provide new reticulation services and/or connections to existing services (e.g. sanitary sewer, storm water, water, electricity and telephone) and also the construction of a shared driveway. The drains have to be constructed to council standards, either as private or public drains. Some work, such as connections to existing public drains, must be done by the council.

✓ *Hazard avoidance/mitigation:*
If the subdivision involves land that is known to the council to be prone to hazards — for example, flooding or land instability — you may be asked to provide a report from an expert. This must outline mitigating measures to ensure the land is safe and suitable for subdivision. Conclusions from the report — such as minimum floor levels, areas in floodplains not suitable for building, or specific foundation design — may be registered on the new title by way of a consent notice.

✓ *Esplanade reserves:*
The council has an obligation under the Resource Management

Act 1991 to require esplanade reserves or strips for public access along coastlines and rivers. If the property you wish to subdivide adjoins a coastline or a river with a bed that has an average width of three metres or more (measured at the annual fullest flow), you will be required to set aside an area 20 metres from the edge of the coastline or river, as an esplanade reserve. This will vest in the council and become part of its parks and reserves network — it cannot be included in the area of any new site, and the value of it cannot be used to reduce any reserve contribution required as part of the subdivision consent.

Step 3: certification of survey plan

Once subdivision consent is granted, you have two years in which to have the section 223 certificate on the survey plan signed by the council. The survey plan, which is legally required to be prepared by a registered surveyor, finalises the area and dimensions of the proposed lots. The section 223 certificate certifies that the plan of the subdivision is approved by the council.

The survey plan is returned to the registered surveyor for lodgement with Land Information of New Zealand (LINZ). LINZ checks the plan to ensure correct definition of boundaries. If satisfactory, the plans are signed 'approved as to survey' by the chief surveyor. A fast track procedure is also available at LINZ for the simultaneous lodgement of the plan and documentation.

Step 4: complete conditions of subdivision consent

You have three years from the date of section 223 certification to get the survey plan deposited by the District Land Registrar, otherwise the subdivision lapses. During this three-year period you need to complete the condition of subdivision consent as outlined in step two above.

If the condition includes engineering works you will need to construct these to council standards. During the construction process, the council will inspect the works.

In subdivisions that involve the construction of public works, you will need to submit engineering plans for council approval before commencing work. This will incur plan approval fees and work supervision charges. You will also have to engage a survey or engineering consultant to supervise the construction and certify that it is completed in accordance with the council's standards.

Once all public engineering works are completed, 'as built' plans must be submitted to the council; these detail final levels and dimensions of construction. The plans are for council records, and the works usually become part of the council's infrastructure.

Step 5: section 224(c) certificate and issue of title

Once you have complied with all the conditions of your subdivision consent, you may request that the council issue the section 224(c) certificate, which certifies that all conditions have been met to the council's satisfaction.

Once all other legal matters have been attended to, such as consent notices, easements and mortgage consents, your solicitor sends the section 224(c) certificate and other documentation to the District Land Registrar. If complete, the survey plan is deposited and the titles are issued for the subdivided lots. The subdivision is now complete.

Costs of subdivision

It is important that all costs associated with a subdivision are budgeted for at the outset. The costs associated with subdivision will vary from property to property but may include:

- ✓ council fees for the subdivision consent application and section 223 and 224(c) certificates
- ✓ council fees for engineering plan approval and works supervision
- ✓ cost of connection to the public infrastructure network
- ✓ costs of extending services for upstream catchments
- ✓ cost for necessary extensions or improvements of the public infrastructure network
- ✓ council fees for a notified land use consent or a non notified land use consent
- ✓ reserve contribution
- ✓ cost of obtaining a valuation for assessing the reserve contribution
- ✓ financial contributions (including the council's solicitor for preparing consent notices, drainage easements, and bond documents) and applicant's solicitor for obtaining the deposit of the survey plan and issue of the new titles
- ✓ construction costs of engineering works (such as driveways, roads, services, etc)
- ✓ fees charged by LINZ
- ✓ surveying and engineering consultants' fees.

12

WRAP Mortgages

WRAP mortgages are a concept that has recently been promoted to New Zealanders, with a corresponding increase in their occurrence. Since WRAPs are becoming more popular, lawyers, accountants, money lenders, the government, the IRD and other organisations have started to pay more attention to them. At the time of publication of this book, the IRD are currently investigating them for tax considerations, mainly GST determinations. Other organisations, such as banks, are still coming to grips with WRAPs, how they work and their implications.

There are many consequences and unknowns about WRAPs. The complicated nature and risks involved in WRAPs mean they are probably not something for novice investors to consider, as they are very different from standard residential property investments. In fact, they are not really a property investment at all, as most of your return comes from you being a money lender.

However, WRAPs provide immediate passive income, and done well, could be a good investment.

How WRAPs operate

A WRAP mortgage is also known as a rent-to-buy option, a lease option, a licence to occupy or an instalment contract.

The scheme is designed around people who would like to own their own home but for one reason or another do not meet normal lending criteria. Because they cannot buy a home in the usual way, an opportunity exists for an investor to sell them a property. The investor buys a property for below its market value and at normal lending rates, and then sells it to the purchaser at a market or slightly higher price, and charges a higher interest rate than he or she is paying for the original mortgage. By creating an income from trading a property for a profit and lending the purchaser the money to buy the property, the investor becomes a property trader and a finance lender.

The property's title remains with the investor until the purchaser completes paying off the loan. This could be for the life of the mortgage, say 25 years, or it could be until the purchaser sells or refinances the property. All expenses — including rates, insurance, maintenance, and so on — are paid by the purchaser as if they were the actual owner.

'Wrapping' is a sophisticated investment, which requires a large investment in contracts, legal and tax advice, and systems and processes. The potential can be attractive. However, if you get your contracts or business processes wrong you can make some very expensive mistakes. The set-up costs for wrapping don't make sense on one or two properties. If you think you are only going to do one or two WRAPs — don't. Stick to rentals.

Advantages of WRAPs

✓ The capital gain on the property is known from the start — that is, the difference between your purchase price and the contract price you have sold the property for.

✓ You have regular cashflow from the beginning and you are not responsible for the usual outgoings, such as rates and maintenance. If the toilet or something else breaks, it is not your responsibility.

✓ Because you are dealing with purchasers, they are generally committed to staying longer than tenants.

✓ There is a potentially high return on investment.

✓ You can make a GST claim on the purchase price of the property and receive the GST portion back straight away.

✓ You retain ownership of the property — unlike a bank, which would have to undertake a mortgagee sale in the event of a default by the purchaser.

Disadvantages of WRAPs

✓ Any increase in property value above the contract sale price belongs to the purchaser. For example, at some time into the agreement, the purchaser finds someone to buy the property for a higher amount than he or she paid you for it. Assuming the amount outstanding is paid back to you, they pocket the difference and the title is then transferred.

✓ There is the potential to taint other current or future investments. This is because, by buying a property with the intention of selling it at a profit plus claiming a GST refund, you will be classed as a trader. This means that other property investments you make will be treated for tax purposes as if they were a development, and you and any related persons selling any property will pay income tax on your profit.

In order to avoid tainting you must have correct structuring and be careful which entities own properties.

✓ Some experts believe you can set up a separate structure for your WRAP investments but others argue this is not enough. Under the IRD's arm's length rules, if you are a director of a company or trustee of a trust involved in property trading, then anything you do under your own name or through another ownership structure is tainted. This could seriously affect your other investments. This is a very complicated area and competent tax and legal advice is essential.

✓ You have to pay back GST on the sale price you have claimed over the life of the scheme (it could be thought of as a long-term loan, however).

✓ You can limit the amount of property you can obtain by running out of equity or cashflow. This can stop you from buying any other rental property.

✓ The purchaser may not keep up insurance and rate payments. If the property is destroyed, you may lose your asset and yet retain the mortgage.

✓ Your sale and purchase agreement could be voided if it is in breach of the Credit Contracts Act. If there are terms in your agreement deemed oppressive — for example, complete forfeiture of all the purchaser's payment in event of default — you may have to repay all the interest you have received from the purchaser.

✓ Banks are wary of WRAPs because if you default on your mortgage, the tenant could frustrate a mortgagee sale due to having signed an Agreement for Sale and Purchase. It is possible that the bank could take over the loan and payments from the purchaser; however, it did not want to do this in the first place and may not want to now. From the bank's point of view you could end up with a mortgage that is higher than the one the purchaser owes you, which increases its risk.

✓ This is a long-term investment. Potentially, a deal may run the full 25 years. You need to have your systems set up to manage the property for the full duration and know that you will still want to actively manage the WRAP for the long term.

✓ The purchaser may default on the agreement and remain in possession. You have to repossess the property under the Property Law Act, not the Residential Tenancies Act, which may take up to two or three months and will involve having to go to court.

✓ Your income is not inflation adjusted. With rental property, rents generally go up by the rate of inflation. Inflation is your enemy with WRAPS as it deteriorates the purchasing power of your fixed income.

✓ You cannot take advantage of leverage – in other words, you cannot use the equity in this property to purchase additional properties.

✓ You are accepting a higher level of risk than the bank is prepared to take by lending to the purchaser.

The process of WRAPs is complicated and not firmly established yet. If you are contemplating beginning an investment in WRAP mortgages then you should seek out independent and professional advice from, at least, your accountant and lawyer.

13

Property Investment Procedures and Tips

Selecting a property

✓ Buy in an area you know very well. Find out about the area from members of the local property investors association, 'To Let' columns in local newspapers, Statistics New Zealand, Quotable Value, local councils, local real estate agents and shopkeepers.

✓ It is easier to manage and keep an eye on a property when it is close to your own home. But if your local area does not meet your requirements (potential capital growth, rental yield, type of property, etc.), consider other areas. You can always use a property manager if the property is in another city or town.

✓ Buy property with a good cashflow (at least a 7% yield, preferably higher), especially if capital growth is likely to be low and/or you are on a low income.

✓ Even though you are buying for the long term, look for areas that are likely to have good capital growth.

✓ Take your time when looking. Property expert Dolf de Roos says you often need to look at 100 properties and put in offers on 10 before you get one great deal.

✓ Low-maintenance cladding, roofing and window joinery reduce time and money spent on repairs.

✓ Multiple-income properties, such as home and income or two properties on one title, tend to offer better rental returns than single houses. Flats usually offer better returns as well.

✓ Houses tend to have higher rental prices than flats, but because flats are generally cheaper than houses they tend to provide better rental yields.

✓ Location is more important than whether the property is a house or a flat — in other words, whether you buy a house or flat is almost immaterial compared with the choice of which area to buy in.

✓ Look for a property with the potential to add value. Can you easily add another bedroom or granny flat? Is it subdividable or cross leaseable? Would it be if you bought some land from the neighbouring property?

✓ Consider how the property will be owned (company, sole trader, partnership, trust, etc.) before you buy.

✓ Consider the type of tenant you are *likely* to get in a property. Are there lots of them? (Not many wealthy people rent.) Do they want to live in this area? Do you want them as tenants?

✓ Organise finance before buying a property so you don't have to make this a condition of purchase.

✓ Use mortgage brokers as their service is free and they can often negotiate a better finance deal than you could on your own.

Negotiating the deal

Just as the top students at school do their homework, the same theory applies in property. Before you get anywhere near negotiating to purchase a property, a smart operator should know as much, if not more, about the property than the current owner. It is then and only then that negotiations should commence.

Through an agent, the current owner will provide quite a few details, like rates, government valuation (GV), DP number, section size, building details, etc, but there is a lot that the current owner may not wish to divulge. With a bit of research, you can uncover information that will strengthen your hand during negotiations. You can use these factors to assist discounting your offer to the vendor.

These factors need not be all negative. Look at all the positive attributes of the property and be prepared for a response on them all, as the vendor or his or her agent will raise them.

The vendor

You need to know the strengths and weaknesses of the vendor. Ask your real estate agent or make discreet inquiries. If the vendor is a company consider doing a credit check and check the companies office records. Better still, ask the tenants.

✓ How long has the vendor owned the property?

✓ If the vendor hasn't owned the property very long, how many owners have there been over the past six years?

✓ Is the vendor financially stretched?

✓ Is the vendor committed to another property and must sell to settle?

✓ Is there a marriage break-up?

✓ Is it a deceased estate that the heirs are squabbling about or live overseas?

✓ Is the vendor prepared to wait for their desired price?

✓ Is there anything the vendor wants that you can easily provide in exchange for a lower purchase price?

The property

Get a LIM report from council as soon as you can. Ask the tenants about the property and the landlord. You will be surprised what they will disclose if you give them leading questions. Information to establish before negotiating:

✓ How long has the property been on the market?

✓ Are the quoted rents realistic or legendary?

✓ Has the property been well maintained? Is it going to need more than a lick of paint?

✓ What is the neighbourhood like?

Property defects

Do your homework and be conscious of any defects in the property. Property inspections are the best way to ensure that you are well informed to commence the negotiations. You need this inspection to be sufficiently informed for the negotiations and an unbiased professional report gives you a lot of negotiating power. The basic things to look for are:

✓ deferred maintenance — for example, rusty leaking spouting, collapsing fences, drab furnishings, etc.

✓ defective title – for example, poorly established right of ways, fences not on boundaries, unsatisfactory common ground on composite titles, etc.

✓ poorly reticulated services – for example, spouting replacement becomes expensive if phone cables are draped inside them, old conduit wiring can set you back thousands

✓ a low rental price for the number of rooms and suburb (this could signify an opportunity or a warning that, for some reason, the property is difficult to let)

✓ paint in poor condition or new paint that comes away easily or is uneven due to poor preparation

✓ cracks in any brickwork, concrete or stucco

✓ cracks in the ceiling and areas of mould indicating leaks, areas of ceiling cleaner than other parts or newly painted

✓ sagging rooflines indicating structural instability.

Handling the negotiation

One of the most important parts of buying a property is negotiating the deal. Dealing directly with a vendor is often difficult. Unless both parties exhibit reasonable negotiation skills the matter goes nowhere. The use of a third party, usually a real estate agent, helps to bring deals together, albeit at a cost. You may choose to use an agent to do this on your behalf (see 'Dealing with Real Estate Agents', pages 134–136). However, the agent primarily works for the vendor, so you need to be a little cautious of this. In reality, the agent is working for a deal to be completed. Agents maximise their income by turning over deals rather than getting the maximum achievable price for individual properties.

Often we come across purchasers who say 'I can't possibly offer such a low price' or 'I don't want to upset the vendor by offering such a low price'. Property investment is a business and you should negotiate the deal like any other business transaction. The vendor doesn't have to accept the deal you offer. If you are not a good negotiator, find someone who can help you out. Good agents are very good negotiators as that is what they do. Alternatively, doing a course on negotiating or reading a book on the subject may be beneficial.

Purchasers and vendors often restrict themselves to negotiating on price. However, there are a number of other things to negotiate on. The best deals need to be good for both parties, and often what is important to one is not as important to the other. Find out if there is any point that is important to the other party that is unimportant to you. Use this unimportant factor to achieve something else that is more important to you. Here are some non-price items that can be used as negotiation points. When negotiating, try and put yourself in the other party's shoes and imagine what they will want.

✓ Find as many points that you can trade with in the negotiation process. Never concede something without trading the concession for something else.

✓ Use facts, such as average rental prices to either strengthen your point or disprove a vendor's point (see rental statistics from *Kiwi Property Investor* magazine).

✓ Try to give flexibility around settlement dates. The vendor may want or need a quick sale, and having a short settlement time may buy you a discount on the price. If you are organised, have done all your checks and have your bank and lawyer ready, you could settle in as little as a week. You may find that the vendor is moving out of town or overseas and thus finds it is attractive to settle quickly.

✓ Have your finance sorted out so you are a cash buyer.

✓ As an investor, the sale is unlikely to be conditional on your selling another property. Making the deal cash or unconditional is a good way to negotiate the price down. However, be extremely careful when you do this. Make sure you have been very thorough in checking out the property and show the deal to your lawyer before you present it.

✓ Although vendor finance is more common in commercial property than residential, it can be useful. You may pay more for a property if the vendor leaves some finance in for say 12 to 24 months.

✓ You may want to rent the house furnished or part furnished and the vendor may be disposing of a lot of furniture. It will be convenient for the vendor not to have to move and then sell the furniture, and it may save you a lot of time and hassle.

✓ Never get angry, upset or frustrated while negotiating. This often leads to a breakdown. If the other side exhibits these emotions, don't be intimidated as you are likely to be close to getting your deal.

✓ There may be some things that need fixing on the property and the vendor is a handyman/builder. You could negotiate for him or her to tidy up a few things in return for your increasing the price you are prepared to pay.

✓ Be prepared to walk away. If you don't have to buy this particular property you are in a stronger bargaining position.

Your first offer

✓ It is not common to put your best offer first. If the vendor accepts your first offer then your investment will work better for you in the future. It is easy to increase your offer price.

✓ Statistics show that on average most properties sell for 8% below their asking price. Your first offer can therefore be a lot lower than this.

✓ Be prepared to justify this first low offer so you do not just appear to be an arrogant bargain hunter, but a reasoned professional who knows what he or she is doing.

Counter offer

✓ Counter offers are common and often affect a number of clauses, not just the purchase price. The first counter offer will give you a sense of the vendor's priorities.

✓ If he or she wants early or late settlement use this to make the deal work for you. For late settlement ask for early access for maintenance and upgrading – which can lead to increased rent and improve the rental yield on purchase. For early settlement, ask for a discounted price.

✓ Most counter offers will produce results that tend to converge on a compromise settlement.

Multi-offer

Avoid multi-offer situations. This is when there is one vendor and several possible purchasers. You can usually expect to pay more. It may be better to accept a conditional offer than counter offer again and find better offers arrive on the table.

Gut feeling

Many business deals are done largely on gut feeling. If, after research and negotiations, the deal looks okay but you have a bad gut feeling, then you either have insufficient confidence or the deal is a dud. It would be best to pull out and start again.

Be patient and careful

Negotiations can sometimes take months to conclude. If you are not patient then you will probably get the short end of the stick.

✓ It is always important to write down what has occurred in negotiations, and this is especially so for long drawn-out negotiations.

✓ Take your time with counter offers presented to you. Remember that the vendor cannot accept other offers if you have been given a counter offer. Be wary, however, that the vendor may be negotiating back-up offers that come into play if you reject or counter offer back again. Alternatively, the vendor could cancel the counter offer if you take too long.

✓ As a general comment, taking your time takes the property off the market and tires out the vendor. But remember that their patience may run out. Make sure that your negotiations do not look like you are playing games.

Mortgagee auctions

These occur typically when an owner of a property defaults on the loan and the bank or finance company auctions the property to recover the amount outstanding on the mortgage. These auctions are very much a case of buyer beware. A couple of things to note are:

✓ Sales are unconditional, with typically a 28-day settlement period and a 10% deposit to pay on the hammer.

✓ Chattels are not included in the sale. This is because the banks do not take the value of chattels into their calculations when deciding how much security they require. Sometimes these are taken when the previous owner leaves.

✓ They are as is where is. This means the current owner may decide to trash the place before leaving (this doesn't happen very often, but it is a risk you take). In most cases, these people are being forced from their home and understandably sometimes they get quite upset.

✓ You are not guaranteed vacant possession, so if the previous owners decide not to leave, the cost and responsibility of evicting them is yours.

✓ Unlike other sales, it is advisable to get insurance cover from the date of the auction, not the settlement date.

Mortgagee auctions can be a good way of finding a deal. When the property market is weak you can find some great deals. However, in strong markets mortgagee sales often go for more than market value, simply because people get caught up in the hype of the market and the emotion on the day.

Another thing to note is that certain real estate companies are extremely good at marketing these mortgagee sales. You will often find it harder to get a bargain when these companies do the auctions.

After buying a rental property

✓ Write your accountant or lawyer a letter stating that your intention for the property is to rent it out as a long-term investment. If it were ever required, this could be used as evidence that stops you being classed as a property trader.

✓ Have a chattels valuation completed. The depreciation rates are higher and you have a better chance of not having to pay back the depreciation you have claimed when you sell the property.

✓ If you will be making a loss on the property get a special tax code using an IR23B so you can access the tax savings every pay day instead of each year at tax return time.

✓ Set up a good filing system.

✓ Get an interest-only mortgage if you have an existing mortgage on your private home. This way all available money will go towards your non tax-deductible home mortgage first.

✓ Set up a bank account for the property to keep it separate from your personal transactions. This makes it much easier to maintain good records.

14

Property Management Procedures and Tips

Knowing the rental market

✓ Check the 'To Let' column of local newspapers.

✓ Go around some properties as a prospective tenant.

✓ Once you know how your property rates (average, below average, above average), keep track of the market rental statistics published in the *Residential Property Investor* magazine.

✓ Review your rental price if the market moves. It is better to lower the rent for a good tenant than risk losing him or her because you become too expensive. On the other hand, failing to raise your rental price reduces your potential investment and can give your tenant a nasty shock when you eventually do raise it.

Promoting your property to let

✓ Most tenants look for properties to rent in the local newspapers.

✓ Most tenants have an area where they want to live in mind, so put that at the start of your advert. After the suburb name, try and start the sentence with an 'A' (e.g. 'A brilliant flat') as most classified adverts are grouped alphabetically and yours will be at or close to the top.

✓ Avoid putting a number after the suburb as these tend to go to the bottom of the list. Check your papers' 'To Let' columns to see whether they are structured differently. Aim to get your advert near the top.

✓ Think of the main benefits your target tenant will want and ensure these are included in your advert. (Young people like big bedrooms, young families like fenced sections. What features will your target tenant most want?)

✓ Putting your mobile phone number instead of your home number gives you privacy and more control over when you speak to prospective tenants, but it can also put prospective tenants off calling. Putting in both numbers means you won't miss any calls should you be away from home.

✓ Print small fliers and put them in letterboxes around the rental property. Often neighbours have friends or relatives who they would like to live nearby or who are looking for a rental home.

✓ Use notice boards at shopping centres, libraries, polytechnics, universities, hospitals, large companies, swimming pools, gyms, etc.

✓ If your departing tenants were good, ask them if they know anyone who would be interested in renting the property.

Screening tenants

Make sure the property is well presented before you show it to anyone.

✓ Minimise 'no-shows' by arranging a specific time to meet the prospective tenants and getting their phone number just in case you need to contact them and change arrangements.

✓ Open rental homes mean you can set the time and duration that you will see tenants. However, you will only see those who can make it at that time. Also, you may get many people turning up at once, which poses a security risk for your departing tenant and means you don't get a good chance to know the prospective tenant.

✓ Write a memory jogger on the rental application form so you can put a face to a name and remember who is who.

✓ Tell interested prospects that you will need to see references from other landlords and make sure you follow these up with a phone call. Tell them that you will check with Baycorp Advantage or some other credit agency.

✓ Ask questions, but don't interrogate them. (Where do they work? How long are they looking to stay in the place? Why are they leaving their old place? What are their interests? How many people will be living in the property? Do they smoke? Can they afford the rent? How many cars do they have?)

✓ Ask all applicants if they are interested before they leave.

✓ If they are interested use a rental application form.

✓ If a prospective applicant isn't interested ask why not in a friendly, interested way. If the property is over priced or has a flaw that can be remedied, it is essential to find out as soon as possible.

✓ If it is not included on the written reference, ask for the previous landlord's contact phone number. Always phone and talk in person – ensure the person really was a past landlord and really meant what was written in the reference.

✓ If you don't get any suitable applicants, don't choose the best of a bad bunch. Keep promoting the property and wait for the first suitable applicant.

Choosing a tenant

✓ Don't be rushed into a decision.

✓ Don't offer the property to the first acceptable tenant. The exception to this is when a tight rental market exists. If you don't use your good judgement you may lose a good tenant to another landlord because you didn't act quickly enough. This does not mean choosing the first prospect who wants the place. First and foremost they must be good tenants.

✓ Don't judge a book by its cover if everything else points to the person being a great tenant.

✓ Don't tell people the property is taken until you have the successful applicant signed up to a tenancy agreement. The applicant may be presented with another offer and change his or her mind.

✓ Remember that you cannot discriminate on the basis of race, gender or age when selecting a tenant and that tenancy agreements with those under 18 must be ratified by Tenancy Services prior to the start of the tenancy (see below).

Signing up a tenant

✓ Do this as soon as you can so you don't lose them to a better offer.

✓ Use a written tenancy agreement. The NZPIF produce a standard form.

✓ Get the tenant's date of birth (useful for finding them if they leave with rent owing), car registration, car licence number (the new photo licences make it easier to verify ownership) and contact details of next of kin.

✓ Get a parental guarantee if the tenant is a student or under 18 years old.

✓ If the tenant is under 18 years old, get Tenancy Services to check the tenancy agreement to ensure it is reasonable. If you don't and a problem occurs, the Tenancy Tribunal could decide that a minor didn't understand a particular part of the agreement and find against you.

✓ If signing up more than one person as a tenant, include the wording 'jointly and severally' after their names. This means if one skips off with money outstanding, the others are responsible for the departing tenant's portion of the rent.

✓ Get the bond payment straight away so you have two weeks' notice should they change their mind before moving in.

✓ Arrange for the rent to be direct credited to your account.

✓ If you have a group flatting situation, insist the tenants make just one rental payment into your bank account rather than paying individually.

✓ Lodge the bond with the Tenancy Services' Bond Centre within 23 working days.

✓ Just before or as the tenants physically take possession of the property, go around together and inspect the property. Note any damage or imperfections on a property inspection form which both parties should sign.

✓ Take photographs or a video of the property at the beginning of the tenancy for the best record of its condition. Use the date function of the video.

✓ Give tenants a tenancy information letter or booklet. Include useful information such as your contact details, what you expect from them as tenants and what they can expect from you as a landlord, what day is rubbish day, contact details for an emergency plumber or builder and how to operate any appliances such as dishwashers.

✓ Introduce the tenants to their new neighbours.

Managing the rental property

✓ Treat your tenants as customers and not mortgage payers. A happy tenant makes for a happy landlord. Be professional and courteous, but you do not need to be the tenants' friend.

✓ If you don't know the neighbours, get to know them. Neighbours can provide an excellent early warning system. Make sure they know how to contact you.

✓ If you don't enjoy managing the property, consider employing a professional property manager.

✓ Join your local property investors association and get the combined experience of all the members.

✓ Conduct regular property inspections at intervals you consider appropriate. You must give at least 48 hours' notice and remember that the tenant is entitled to quiet enjoyment of the property.

✓ When conducting inspections take the opportunity to look for items that need repair as well as checking how the tenant is keeping the property.

✓ Respond to repairs as quickly as you can.

✓ If your insurance policy has any special requirements, ensure that you are meeting them.

✓ Keep a close eye on rent payments, especially in the first three months. Check rents have been paid the day they should have been. (Telephone and internet banking facilities help.)

✓ Write a welcome letter after the first rental payment has been made. Tell them you received the rental payment and assure them the system is working. This also shows you're on the ball.

✓ Be firm, fair and fast when dealing with missed rental payments. The last is probably more important.

When a tenant leaves

✓ Don't accept the bond as the last rent payment. This is your security should you find a problem with the tenancy or property. If you have allowed the tenants to use the bond as their last rent payment then you have given away your security.

✓ Write a confirmation letter thanking them for being good tenants, confirm the date they are leaving, confirm the condition you want the place left in and when the property inspection will occur.

✓ Conduct a property inspection together once all their property has been removed.

✓ Release the bond money when you have checked everything out.

✓ Give them a written reference and ask them for one regarding your performance as a landlord. In a tight rental market you can use this to help secure a new tenant.

15

When Things Go Wrong with a Tenancy

Good tenant screening, keeping a close eye on rent payments and regular inspections are your best defence against things going wrong. However, problems can occur even in an actively managed rental property.

The Tenancy Tribunal has been established to handle disputes between landlords and tenants.

Residential Tenancies Act 1986

This is a comprehensive act of parliament, which provides all the rules and information about residential tenancies. You do not need to look anywhere else for information or authority. It is self-contained.

What are the benefits of the Residential Tenancies Act?

✓ It provides advice for landlords and tenants.

✓ Applications can be completed and filed by landlords with no need for lawyers.

✓ Mediation is provided as part of the dispute resolution service.

✓ Reasonably quick hearing times.

✓ Bond holding by Tenancy Services offsets the cost of dispute resolution.

✓ Provides an adjudicator as the final arbiter of disputes.

Who operates the system?

✓ *Tenancy Services:*

Tenancy Services are responsible for administering the service as a whole, in particular providing that advice to both parties, mediation to both parties, serving applications on the parties, issuing notices of hearing and providing forms and written information. The local office of the Tenancy Services is listed in your telephone directory.

✓ *Tenancy Tribunal:*

This is independent of Tenancy Services and is administered through the Department for Courts.

It is often thought that Housing New Zealand is part of the Tenancy Services system. Housing New Zealand is the name of the organisation that manages all the state rental units and was formerly known as Housing Corporation. It is often confused with one or other of the above, but plays no part at all in the system.

Mediation

Mediation is an alternative method of dispute resolution in which a trained mediator employed by Tenancy Services contacts the parties and invites them to a facilitated discussion. The hope is that by talking through the issues in a non-confrontational way, the parties can resolve the dispute themselves.

✓ Mediation should be tried first as a preliminary way of resolving a dispute.

✓ Mediation is voluntary and cannot take place without your presence. You cannot be compelled to attend. Both landlord and tenant have rights to expect certain things will happen in mediation and these are set out below.

The parties' rights in mediation

✓ To have the issues in your application thoroughly canvassed.

✓ To not have other litigious issues raised by the mediator without those issues being the subject matter of an application or without your prior consent.

✓ To be given a full, free and uninterrupted opportunity to have your say.

✓ To have the grounds set before the mediation gets started and to have the mediator enforce them fairly.

✓ To be treated with courtesy and respect by the mediator and the other party.

✓ To have any agreement sealed as of right. (Once sealed, the agreement is binding and enforceable just as if it were made in the Tenancy Tribunal.)

✓ To have a consequential clause inserted to make the agreement 'have teeth'.

✓ To have the mediator act at all times in a fair and even-handed manner.

Tenants' rights

The Residential Tenancies Act 1986 sets out a number of rights of tenants.

✓ Tenants have the right to enjoy peace, privacy and comfort in the use of the tenancy premises.

✓ Tenants have the right to expect that the landlord will not come onto the rental property or into the rental premises other than as permitted by the Residential Tenancies Act.

✓ Tenants have the right to expect that when they take occupation of rental premises that the premises will be reasonably clean and tidy.

✓ Tenants have the right to expect that the landlord will complete maintenance and repairs in a timely manner and that urgent repairs will be completed urgently — for example, failed hot water cylinder.

✓ Tenants have the right to not have the landlord interfere with any essential services, such as water, gas or electricity.

✓ Tenants have the right to compel landlords to carry out necessary maintenance by applying to the Tenancy Tribunal for a 'work order'.

✓ Tenants have the right to expect that the premises will at all times be safe to live in and comply with all health and safety requirements. The premises must also be reasonably secure (capable of being locked up).

✓ Tenants can expect that the landlord will not change or alter any of the locks at the tenancy premises unless such change is with the tenants' consent.

✓ Tenants have the right to expect that when a tenancy agreement provides for occupation on a particular day that the tenants will have occupation on that day.

✓ Tenants have the right to possess a copy of a written tenancy agreement before the tenancy commences. The tenancy agreement must contain certain minimum information, including the contact address of the landlord.

✓ Notwithstanding the requirement to have tenancy agreements in writing, tenants can still enforce the terms of any oral agreement entered into between the landlord and tenant.

✓ Tenants have the right to receive written notice of any rent increase and such notice shall be at least 60 days' notice in writing and not more frequently than every 180 days or from the beginning of a new tenancy.

✓ Tenants have the right to challenge the rent being charged by the landlord if they believe that the rent they are paying is substantially in excess of the market rent.

✓ Tenants can expect that the landlord will keep adequate business records, in particular records of rent payments and any bond payments.

✓ Tenants cannot be required to pay rent more than fortnightly in advance and cannot be required to pay rent for any period for which rent has already been paid.

✓ Tenants cannot be required to pay a tenancy bond of more than the equivalent of four weeks' rent. The bond must be held by Tenancy Services.

✓ Tenants entering tenancy agreements cannot be charged any

fee or charge other than a letting fee by a real estate agent or a fee by a solicitor.

✓ Tenants have the right not to be charged penalty rent if they are late paying rent but if rent is discounted for any reason then they shall be entitled as of right to pay the discounted amount of rent.

✓ Tenants have the right to apply to the Tenancy Tribunal to shorten a fixed-term tenancy but they must show: unforeseen circumstances at the time the agreement was entered into, and that their hardship is greater than the landlord's hardship.

✓ Tenants have the right to receive at least 90 days' written notice by the landlord to terminate the tenancy unless the landlord has a reason justifying a shorter notice of 42 days.

✓ Tenants have the right to give 21 days' notice to terminate a periodic tenancy, at any time.

✓ Tenants have the right to not have their goods or personal effects seized by the landlord. (This does not apply to enforcement proceedings.)

Unlawful acts

Throughout the Residential Tenancies Act there are a number of acts and omissions which are categorised as 'unlawful acts'.

✓ Tenants have the right to bring an application against the landlord for any breach of an unlawful act and on adequate proof, to receive an award for exemplary damages.

✓ Tenants have the right to claim compensation from the landlord where the landlord has committed a breach of the tenancy agreement or any of the provisions of the Residential Tenancies Act.

✓ If the landlord decides to sell the property, then the tenant has the right to receive a notice advising him or her that the property is on the market for sale.

✓ Tenants can expect that the landlord will contact them and negotiate access to the rented premises for the purposes of showing the premises to prospective tenants or purchasers.

✓ When the property is sold with vacant possession, tenants can expect to receive not less than 42 days' notice in writing to terminate the tenancy.

✓ Tenants have the right to expect that any personal effects left at the end of a tenancy and of some value will be secured by the landlord and only be disposed of by order of the Tenancy Tribunal (see 'Two common problem areas', pages 119-122).

✓ Tenants have the right to challenge any notice to terminate the tenancy issued by the landlord if at the same time the tenant is exercising a right against the landlord. This means that if the tenant brings up an issue with the landlord, the landlord cannot simply evict the tenant to avoid having to deal with the issue — this is considered retaliatory.

✓ Tenants and prospective tenants must not be subjected to unlawful discrimination.

✓ Tenants have the right not to be arbitrarily or capriciously evicted. The tenant has the right to challenge any acts or omissions of the landlord in the Tenancy Tribunal. (Evictions can only be effected by bailiffs and only after due process in the Tenancy Tribunal.)

Landlords' rights

Landlords have many rights in respect of the tenancy and the tenant. The basic landlord rights are:

✓ to have problems resolved quickly and efficiently using the Tenancy Services system

✓ to have the problem mediated to conclusion if you choose

✓ to apply to the Tenancy Tribunal to resolve a dispute

✓ to obtain orders that terminate the tenancy and other orders for money as compensation.

Two common problem areas

The range of potential problems is wide and varied. The two most common areas of dispute are tenants not paying the rent and damage to the property. Not paying the rent falls into two main categories: missing a payment but wanting to stay, or leaving without any notice.

1. Not paying rent

Missed payment:

As soon as you identify a rent payment has been missed, issue your tenant with a 10-day notice to remedy (for a free standard form see www.propertyinvestor.info and go to downloads). The 10-day letter is your fastest way to get a Tenancy Tribunal hearing. If issued the day after the rent was due to be paid, you can apply to the Tribunal for eviction 10 days later, rather than having to wait three weeks.

However, if this is an isolated incident, talk to your tenants first and ascertain why the rent wasn't paid. If there was a legitimate reason, they had been tenants for a reasonable period and they were previously reliable, then work out a way for the missed rent to be repaid.

Get the tenants back to paying the full rent for the next period. Do not let the issue get confused by paying a little of the missed rental period and a little of the current rental period.

If they break the agreement, invoke the 10-day letter and apply for a Tenancy Tribunal hearing. Ask for urgency as they are a sitting tenant.

Tenant leaves without notice:

Although it may sound crazy, if a tenant leaves without notice, you need to apply to the Tribunal to end the tenancy and gain possession of your property.

One of the biggest problems are items left behind by the tenants. These abandoned goods have caused problems for landlords in more ways than one.

Firstly, remember that one person's trash is another's treasure and assume that the goods left behind are all cherished possessions of your departing tenants. If you know where the tenants are or how to get hold of them, ask them to come and get the items. Give them a reasonable time in which to do so and hopefully the problem will resolve itself. Informing the tenants' family or friends may also get the message to the tenants.

If this doesn't sort things out, and you have legal possession of the property, you can throw out any food or goods that are perishable. Other items should be safely stored and an application made to the Tenancy Tribunal for an order to dispose of them. Once you have an order it will protect you against any claims that you stole the goods made by your departed tenants at a later stage.

This has happened and the landlord, not being able to produce the items, has lost.

The Tribunal can make several orders about tenants' possessions. It can make an order to get rid of the goods. It can order that the tenants get the goods back, or that someone else can have the goods if they can prove ownership. It can order that goods of no value be dumped. With items of value, the Tribunal can order that the landlord sells them at the best price available and the money is held by the Bond Centre. The Tribunal can also order that the proceeds from the sale of the goods be used to offset any claims that the landlord may have against the tenants.

If the Tribunal orders that the landlord is owed some money by the tenants, and the bond does not cover this amount, then money from the abandoned goods can also be paid out to the landlord to make up the difference. Any money left can be claimed by the tenants within a year.

You can still claim the bond, and the bond can also be used if there were no proceeds from the sale but costs were incurred in getting rid of the abandoned goods.

This does involve effort for the landlord but, handled in the right way, goods left behind by tenants need not cause future problems and aggravation.

2. Damage to rental property

If there is a dispute over damage to the property, the chance of receiving compensation will depend a lot on your record keeping. The two key factors you will need to prove is that the damage occurred during the tenancy and that it was beyond reasonable wear and tear.

Conducting a property inspection with new tenants immediately before they move in and giving them a copy with both your signatures on it is imperative. This can prove that the damage was not there before the tenant moved in. If the tenants have moved out of the premises, you need to conduct a property inspection immediately after they have moved out and before you take possession. That way you can prove that the damage occurred during the tenancy.

Fair wear and tear is not so cut and dry, as it can be an arbitrary decision. Stains on carpets are often the main problem. Accidents do happen, so is the odd stain merely to be expected or is it damage over and above reasonable wear and tear? Before and after photographs or videos with the date recorded on them are a good way to show that the damage was beyond fair wear and tear.

Applying to the Tenancy Tribunal

You can obtain the necessary forms from Tenancy Services. There is a $20 filing fee that is payable at any Westpac bank, where your forms will be stamped when you pay the fee.

Whether you are making an application for mediation or for a Tribunal hearing, it is important that the application form you fill out is clear and thorough and includes all the relevant information. (It is the same as having clear, easily understood rent records and a signed tenancy agreement.) This shows you are running your business professionally and avoids delays in getting your application processed.

The most common types of landlord applications

1. If the tenant is more than 21 days in arrears with the rent as at the date of application, use the simple wording suggested below.

Orders requested

Order for termination of tenancy (Section 55).

Order for vacant possession to the landlord.

Order for payment of rent arrears to date of termination.

Order for release of the bond of $..... to the applicant.

Reasons

Rent is in arrears by more than 21 days and is only paid up to .... (*fill in the date*).

Note: Do not include rent in advance. The arrears cannot include any money due for rent beyond the date your application is lodged with Tenancy Services. Rent can be reassessed at the date of mediation or termination.

2. If you have sent a 10-working-day notice to remedy and it has expired unremedied, ask for termination under section 56. (Section 56 is for when rent is less than 21 days in arrears, but a 10-working-day notice was sent, has now expired, but has not been remedied.) Use the simple wording suggested below.

Orders requested

Order for termination of tenancy (Section 56).

Order for vacant possession to the landlord.

Order for payment of rent arrears to date of termination.

Order for release of the bond of $..... to the applicant.

Reasons
A 10-working-day notice was sent. It has now expired, but has not been remedied. Rent is now in arrears by $..... and is only paid up to ...... (*fill in date*).

3. If you are applying for compensation after the tenancy has been vacated, apply under Section 77. Once you have an itemised list already prepared and an accurate assessment of the amount you will claim for each item, you can ask for an order for compensation for cleaning and repairs to the tenancy. The list could include specific amounts for: cleaning, removal of rubbish, reglazing windows, changing locks, and a total cost. State the date the tenancy was vacated and ask for any of the relevant orders listed below.

    Orders requested
    Order for payment of rent arrears to date of termination.

    Order for compensation for cleaning and repairs, lock change, rubbish removal, etc.

    Order for release of the bond of $..... to the applicant.

4. If you are applying for possession because you are sure the tenancy has been abandoned, apply under Section 61. (You can do a 'monthly' property inspection 48 hours after placing a written notice on the door of the tenancy, then secure the premises and lock up any abandoned goods until you get the disposal order.)

Write out the application using the simple wording suggested below:

Orders requested
Order for termination of tenancy (Section 61).

Order for vacant possession to the landlord.

Order for disposal of abandoned goods.

Order for payment of rent arrears to date of termination.

Order for payment of rent in lieu of notice (for periodic tenancy).

Order for release of the bond of $..... to the applicant.

Reasons
Property abandoned.

(Give brief details as to evidence of abandonment.)

Enforcement

A successful Tribunal decision is just half the battle. You now have to get the money from the tenant.

At the end of the mediation or Tribunal hearing the mediator may write an order or report recording the agreement that has been reached. The order may say what one or both parties will do (such as paying rent arrears or making repairs), and what will happen if they don't (such as the tenancy being terminated).

If one party has not done what the order said, the other party can start the procedure to enforce the order known as enforcement proceedings. (It may still be worthwhile, however, for the parties to try and talk about the issue to settle it.)

If the Tenancy Tribunal has not already sealed the order, then ask Tenancy Services to have this done so that enforcement can proceed. This must be done within six months of the date on the order. A mediated agreement that is sealed by the Tenancy Tribunal becomes an order of the Tenancy Tribunal that is enforceable.

At all stages of the enforcement process a current address must be provided for the person against whom the order is made. A current address allows the Collections Unit of the Department for Courts to locate the person. The Collections Unit does not have any other way of finding the person to enforce your order. Alternatively, a debt collection agency could be used. A debt collection agency may have the debt repaid but cannot enforce a possession order.

The following are different types of enforcement orders and the fees that are chargeable. All fees paid for enforcement are recoverable from the debtor.

Possession order (eviction)

A possession order allows the landlord to repossess his or her property. An application for a possession order must be made within three months of a termination order. The fee is $55. Complete the application for a possession order and give the Collections Unit the following items:

✓ the Tenancy Tribunal order or the sealed mediator's order

✓ a copy of the notice terminating the tenancy

✓ a current address of the person who owes the money.

A collections officer will contact the landlord to arrange a time for the enforcement of the possession order. The landlord must be at the premises at this agreed time. It is a good idea for the landlord to arrange for a locksmith to be present at the same time to change the locks so that the premises are secure.

Money orders

The most common means of enforcing money orders are issuing a distress warrant or an order for examination.

Distress warrant

The fee for a distress warrant is $55. A distress warrant enables the Collections Unit to make a demand of the other person for the money owed or to report on assets that can be taken and sold by the Collections Unit to pay the money owed to the applicant. A distress warrant is only useful if the Collections Unit is satisfied that the other person has assets of sufficient value that can be sold to pay the money owed.

Complete the application for a distress warrant and give the Collections Unit the following items:

✓ the Tenancy Tribunal order or the sealed mediator's order

✓ a current address of the person who owes the money.

Order for examination

The fee for an order for examination is $90. A registrar of the District Court can make this order if the debtor (the person who owes the money) has the means to pay.

Complete the application for an order for examination and give the Collections Unit the following items:

✓ the Tenancy Tribunal order or the sealed mediator's order

✓ a deposit slip for your bank account

✓ a current address of the person who owes the money.

An order for examination summons the debtor to appear before the registrar. The applicant will be notified of the hearing date and must attend the hearing. At the hearing the registrar will ask the debtor to provide evidence of assets and liabilities, and repayment options will be discussed. The registrar will make an order for the repayment of the debt, usually by instalments. Payments can be ordered to be made by: automatic payment to the applicant; payment into the court; or an order on a benefit, wages or salary (known as an attachment order). If the debtor does not attend the hearing, the applicant will be asked if they require a warrant of arrest to be issued.

17

Selecting Property Experts

It is important that the professionals you use to provide advice are able to work in a team environment. This ensures a complete exchange of information between the various consultants.

Having the right team of professionals will ensure that all aspects of your property investment are correctly structured to work together producing the best long-term results.

Cost benefits can also be achieved by retaining the services of experienced practitioners who can, for example, prepare their invoices to you in a manner that allows their costs to be deductible as legitimate expenses.

It is essential to surround yourself with a team of good professionals to help you with your property business. The team may include:

✓ an accountant

✓ a lawyer

✓ an independent mortgage broker

✓ two valuers (one for buying, one for selling)

✓ a builder

✓ a plumber

✓ an electrician

✓ a painter

✓ a cleaner

✓ several real estate agents (again, some for buying, some for selling)

✓ a property manager.

Property matters are specialised and you need a specialist to give you the correct advice. This is especially true of your accountant and lawyer. With the exception of the cleaner and possibly the tradespeople, it is essential that the members of your team are either property investors themselves or specialise in property investment. This counts for the real estate agents as well. Don't think that they will always take the best deals for themselves.

If you choose to use a property manager, then you won't need the tradespeople as part of your team as the property manager will handle these aspects of your investment.

When looking for specialists, ask a couple of questions in addition to the common questions relevant to their profession such as:

✓ Do they specialise in property investment?

✓ How many property investors do they have as clients?

✓ Are they property investors themselves?

✓ What are their qualifications and experience?

✓ Are they a member of an industry or professional body?

✓ Could you see referrals from someone they know?

✓ Are they giving independent advice?

Selecting a property manager

When using a property manager it is essential that you are careful and selective over whom you use. A first step in selecting a property manager is to contact some over the phone and review the information afterwards. Questions to ask are:

✓ How long have you been in the property management industry?

✓ What qualifications, training and experience do you have?

✓ Are you full- or part-time?

✓ What back up is there for when you are sick or on leave?

✓ What systems do you have for managing the properties?

✓ What areas do you cover?

✓ What services are provided?

✓ What is the fee structure, including base fee and additional charges?

From the information provided by each of them, produce a shortlist and meet each of these managers face to face. Property managers must have excellent people skills, which simply cannot be identified through notes or a phone conversation.

In evaluating a potential property manager, keep in mind that the individual is more important than the company for which he or she works. The manager plays a critical part in correct tenant selection, ability to communicate plus responsiveness to both tenant and owner requests.

Some points to cover in the interview are:

✓ Ask about their rental payment tracking and view their computer and/or book-keeping system.

✓ Ask to see a sample inspection form and the type of comments being recorded. Such a set of records can save a lot a hassle when it comes time to end a tenancy. They are also a very useful tool for recording agreed actions each time an inspection takes place.

✓ Ask about their fee structure, which will vary between companies. The main thing to ensure is that all fees are clearly explained so there are no hidden surprises further down the track. You need to ask whether they charge for each inspection (including entry/exit inspections, bond inspections, repairs completed by tradespeople, and so on), if they charge a fee for arranging repairs and maintenance, charges for advertising, administration and credit checks.

✓ Find out what process they use for tenant selection, plus the types of checks they carry out on interested parties. This should at least include credit checks, references and a phone call to the potential tenants' previous landlord.

✓ Ask the property manager what type of problems they have had with tenants in the past and what they have done to ensure that similar things don't happen again.

✓ Ask them for references from property owners for whom they are currently working. *

Once you have produced a shortlist of potential managers, it is useful to talk to a selection of the property owners they are currently working for. This type of feed-back is really important and it only takes a few phone calls. It is important to note that taking on a property manager is like hiring an employee in your business, and should be given the same serious consideration.

18

Dealing with Real Estate Agents

Working with good real estate agents is extremely important. One of the most time-consuming components of property investment is finding the right property to buy. A good agent, especially one that understands investment property, can save you a lot of time.

You make your money when you buy, so take time to make sure you buy well. This can be very challenging when the market is strong and, although easier when the markets are weak, it requires a strong stomach to buy when most others are staying well clear.

In the last 10 years, approximately 50% of new salespeople have left the industry after only one year and a further 45% in their second year, leaving only a few who have been around more that two years. It's a tough industry to be in with long hours worked and only about 30% earn more than $40,000 per annum.

You often hear comments about how bad real estate agents are. And yes, as in any industry, there are some bad ones. But there are also a lot of purchasers who are extremely hard to deal with. It is a two-way street and you need to develop a good relationship with your agent, just as you do any other professional. You may like to ask for client references.

What to look for in an agent

✓ Have they been in the industry for more than three years?

✓ How much experience have they had selling investment properties and dealing with investors?

✓ Do they seem professional, efficient and well organised?

✓ How are they ranked within their office and/or company and area in terms of sales?

✓ Do they have good local knowledge?

✓ Can they provide you with evidence of their recent sales?

✓ Do you feel comfortable with them and can you communicate well with them?

What you need to do

✓ Do your homework and understand what you are looking for in an investment property.

✓ Have some guidelines to give the agent so it is clear what you want.

✓ Be ready to buy – that is, have your financing pre-approved.

✓ Establish information sources so you know the market well and can confidently establish property and rental values for properties you view.

✓ Have an established relationship with a lawyer.

✓ Be professional.

✓ Be honest with the agent and give feedback to him or her.

✓ Have good systems in place so you can efficiently evaluate properties.

✓ Be responsive and get back to your agent quickly.

✓ In a strong sellers' market, keep in contact with your agents so you remain in their mind.

Real estate agents work on commission and therefore get paid only if they get the sale. Be organised and know what you want. Don't muck them around and waste their time. Treat them as you would like to be treated and you are a long way towards developing a good working relationship. Remember, you want the agents to call you first before they call others so that you have first option on the deal.

19

Property Software

PC Property Manager v2 by Estatement

www.PCPropertyManager.com

PC Property Manager aims to save residential property investors time and money by streamlining record keeping, better rental tracking and lower accounting fees.

It allows multiple ownership structures, multiple properties and bank accounts, and links tenants to properties and calculates when rent is due and outstanding rents.

It calculates depreciation, records 'to let' advertisements and has a reminder system of things to do (check rent, property inspections, and so on).

Receipts and payments are easily entered from one screen with various features to make data entry quick and simple.

All ledger accounts can be fully customised so you can adapt the system to your own requirements.

A contact system allows you to keep track of all phone calls and correspondence in connection with the property, including contacts to and from tenants, tradespeople, etc. A diary of contacts can be easily printed out for potential use in the Tenancy Tribunal. Depreciation of building and chattels is easily entered into the system and automatically updates each year without having to re-enter the amount depreciated.

A large range of reports allow for income and expenditure, profit and loss, key performance indicators and many other reports to be filtered by owner, property, tenant or date range. Reports can be exported in a variety of ways to be given to your accountant or tax advisor.

The package costs NZ$225 and can be ordered by email (sales@PCPropertyManager.com) or writing to Estatement Ltd, PO Box 44–196, Auckland.

Property Investment Analysis (PIA) software

The Property Investment Analysis (PIA) program is an essential decision tool for all property investors. It quickly and easily tells you whether a property fits your buying criteria and helps to show the outcome of planned improvements you could make to the property. PIA will analyse the capital growth, cash flows, and tax implications for any investment property and provide instant feedback on the projected after-tax cost and rate of return.

The software computes cash-flow projections for up to 40 years and has facilities for changing more than 100 variables including property price, rent, capital growth, inflation, deposit, loan type, etc. The internal rate of return (IRR) and the cost-per-week are recalculated automatically whenever a change is made.

PIA Personal Professional is a powerful analysis tool for investors who want all the extra functionality of the Professional version, but for personal use only. This version has all the features listed above, plus additional spreadsheets for home-loan analysis, linked loan analysis, and a wealth builder for interactively building a property portfolio over a number of years. It also has extensive graphics, a suite of property and finance calculators, and a much wider array of report options. This version has a single-user licence, and is restricted to personal use. This essential tool is now available in New Zealand for just $295 including GST. This is a greatly reduced price.

PIA Professional is for industry professionals who want to use PIA to help investors understand all the benefits and implications of investing in property. This version has all the features of the PIA Personal Professional plus additional client-related features (e.g. client detail fields and professional disclaimers in any generated reports). The professional package also includes a site licence for the software. This version of PIA is available to industry professionals for $595 including GST.

20

Useful Websites

Estatement (PC Property Manager)

www.PCPropertyManager.com

Website of a New Zealand-developed property management software. Free download is available. It is easy to set up, offers quick and easy financial recording, and is good for keeping track of rent payments and a reminder system.

Dolf de Roos

www.dolfderoos.com

Website of New Zealand's best-known property expert. Dolf de Roos provides a monthly column and information on his speaking schedule and property school. The site also covers his books, tapes, software products and property ventures, plus his property company that you can invest in.

New Zealand Property Investors Federation

www.nzpif.org.nz

The official website of the New Zealand Property Investors Federation. It includes information on the federation and contact details for all associations around the country; access to an electronic form of the Residential Tenancies Act; and products and publications for sale, including tenancy agreements.

Kiwi Property Investor magazine

www.kpimagazine.co.nz

Website of the monthly magazine. Offers subscriptions, details the current issue and catalogues articles from back issues.

Real Estate Institute of New Zealand

www.realenz.org.nz

Website of the Real Estate Institute. It advertises properties for sale all over the country. Searches can be filtered geographically, by price, by property, home and income, number of rooms, etc.

QV on-line

www.quotable.co.nz

Website of Quotable Value NZ Ltd, a valuation company that was previously the government's Valuation Department. For a fee, it can provide online estimates of property values as well as statistics on recent property sales. The site explains rating valuations and how to object to a rating valuation.

Real estate for sale

www.realestate.co.nz

The website of a group of agencies: Barfoot and Thompson, Harveys, Harcourts, Ray White, L. J. Hooker, Leaders, Century 21 and Bayleys. Select from houses, units, commercial or land, and filter by area.

Baycorp Advantage

www.baycorp.co.nz

You can obtain free membership to Baycorp Advantage by becoming a member of the New Zealand Property Investors

Federation. The website gives you access to most Baycorp services. This includes credit checks on potential tenants, and information on properties or cars you are looking to buy.

Empower Education

www.empowereducation.com

Resource website including books, software and seminars for all types of investments and investors.

Good Returns

www.goodreturns.co.nz

An online business news service, which has a mortgage information section that includes some property information. The main focus is on financial products rather than property.

Tenancy Services

www.minhousing.govt.nz/tenancy/index.html

Includes information on the Tenancy Tribunal, an electronic version of the Residential Tenancies Act 1986, and some tenancy forms.

Property Returns

www.propertyreturns.co.nz

A general website for property investors. It has an online discussion forum and a find-a-tradesperson section.

21

Book Reviews

The New Zealand Investor's Guide to
Making Money in Residential Real Estate
Jan Somers and Dolf de Roos
This is the book that is often credited with an explosion of property investors in New Zealand — although in truth they were always there. But this was the first book to be written from a New Zealand perspective. It was first published in 1992 and was updated for the 11th time in January 2000.

It is a short and snappy, easy-to-read book which focuses on 'why' invest and strategies to invest rather than management of property. The main sections of the book cover finance and tax implications. It covers the basic principles of property investment, suggests you have a sound asset backing, reasonable cashflow and knowledge.

It is an inspiring book that is just as popular today as it was a decade ago.

Building Wealth Through Investment Property
Jan Somers and Dolf de Roos
A larger version of *Making Money in Residential Real Estate*, this book expands on some of the information presented in that guide, and concentrates more on setting goals and developing the right attitude to succeed in property investment.

It compares property with other investment classes, as well as looking at different forms of property investment and what to look for in a residential rental property, how to develop wealth creation strategies and the tools — such as knowledge of interest rates, borrowing costs, finance, tax deductions, and the buying and selling process — you will need to achieve your goals. Once you have generated wealth the book looks at ways to keep it.

Extraordinary Profits from Ordinary Properties
Dolf de Roos

A collection of inspirational stories from New Zealand property investors — certainly not an academic review of how to and how not to invest in real estate. The story is told in the words of real New Zealanders telling of how they made extraordinary profits from essentially ordinary properties. One story is of a solo parent who bought a property with 100% financing. It was positively geared from day one and in 18 months provided the owner with a tax-free capital growth of $35,000. More than just about how they did it, the book is inspirational in that it illustrates how investors took the time to get out there and make something happen.

Landlording in New Zealand:
A complete manual for rental property owners
Frank Saxton

This is a book with good practical tips on how to get the best out of your investment property. It discusses how to buy a property and sort out the tax situation. However, the main emphasis is on how to set up your investment to maximise the return you will get from it and minimise the amount of time you will have to spend on it. Once you have correctly set the property up, Saxton talks about how to find tenants and provides a guide to the Residential Tenancies Act, the Bond Centre and the Tenancy Tribunal. There is a section on rent, which covers how to set the rent, methods of collection, initiating rent increases, communicating with your tenant about rent issues and how to handle rent arrears. The book concludes with sections on keeping good records, preparing tax returns and property maintenance.

Real Estate Riches
Dolf de Roos

This is part of Robert Kiyosaki's 'Rich Dad's Advisors' series, a collection of books written by the individuals that Kiyosaki uses to advise him in different areas of business and investment. It is high praise that he has chosen New Zealander Dolf de Roos to write on investment property. (In the foreword Kiyosaki refers to de Roos as 'one of the greatest teachers of real estate in the world'.)

Rather than a book on the mechanics of investment property, de Roos discusses why he believes property is such a good investment and shares his approach, attitudes, techniques and secrets. These are presented on a strategic rather than logistic level, and will challenge seasoned investors as well as novices. The aim of this book is to get the readers to work out the most appropriate method for their particular circumstances.

A key point made in the book is for investors to beat the average. De Roos gives reasons why one area will increase in value above that of another — for instance, you have a better chance of getting higher property prices in an area where more jobs are being created, has an increasing population or a better climate —

showing you how to evaluate areas to invest in.

If you are going to evaluate a lot of properties to buy just one, then you need a good system to do this. De Roos explains why he believes yield calculations are not the optimal way to evaluate property as they don't paint a complete picture. He suggests cash-on-cash and internal-rate-of-return methods are better tools, and explains how they work.

In the final chapters, de Roos presents his eight golden rules learned through study and his own experiences of investment property.

The New Zealand Landlord's Handbook
Frank Newman and Suzi Bilosh

Newman has owned rental property for many years and has written nine other books, including *Making Money on the New Zealand Share Market*. This book focuses on the day-to-day management of rental property, providing systems with detailed information on how to operate your rental property in a professional manner. The book is presented in a logical format, with chapters covering finding the right tenant, starting a tenancy, managing the tenancy, when the tenancy ends and extra information on investment property. This includes taking care of your investment, record keeping and taxation.

The part of the book covering property management is the longest section. It is broken down into four sub-sections covering common questions from landlords, tenancy law, problem solving and notices to tenants. The various steps of tenant/landlord conflict resolution are also presented if a solution to the problem cannot be reached. This involves an overview of how to prepare for the Tenancy Tribunal. A range of notices are presented covering issues such as rent arrears, property inspections, rent increases and a questionnaire for outgoing tenants.

Having read *The New Zealand Landlord's Handbook*, a newcomer to the industry would have an excellent overview of what to do when starting out.

Mortgage Concepts to Enhance Wealth Creation
Kieran Trass

This is directed more towards property investors than home owners. Trass has been involved in the finance industry for over 18 years and is currently general manager of Mortgagenet. The focus is on the newer mortgage structures and concepts: they are presented in an easy-to-comprehend manner with advice on how they work, when they are best used and who they best suit.

The much-debated topic of whether an investor should repay principal and interest or just the interest on their investment loan is covered. Trass believes that it depends on individual circumstances, attitudes to risk and property investment goals.

The concept of 'interest rate averaging', which Trass developed in response to fluctuating mortgage interest rates and the difficulty in predicting the timing and direction of their movements, is described in the guide.

Many investors break fixed-term rates when floating rates are low, then fix them again when the rates appear to rise. Trass believes this strategy is a short-term solution to a long-term (mortgage) commitment, involving high stress levels and low odds on making the right decision for any great length of time. Trass also discusses revolving credit mortgages, how they work and when they are unsuitable. Although widely used overseas, mortgage broking is a relatively new concept in New Zealand and Trass looks at its likely direction in this country and what to look for in a mortgage broker.

The book ends with a section on risk analysis for property investors and details on independent sources of information to help you keep up to date with your property industry knowledge. Enquiries on the book can be made by phoning 09-638-3350.

Lost Property
Olly Newland

Newland's classic book has been revised and updated, with four new chapters added to the original version written in 1993. The book reads like a ripping yarn from an old boy's own annual. The difference is that the names of the characters are all well known, the scene is set in New Zealand — not some faraway country — and it isn't fiction but an account of actual events that changed our nation.

It is not written from an academic point of view but by one of the key players involved in the highs and lows of those dramatic days. From Newland's words, you get an insight into his thoughts and feelings and not just a record of events and their outcomes. Newland doesn't just point out the good parts, however. He frankly describes his own personal weaknesses and mistakes, including a lack of knowledge about the sharemarket and how to run a large company.

Many personal insights are provided as Newland starts to buy property and builds up his new empire. He became obsessed with Landmarks share price and at times didn't understand the motives behind movements in the price.

He describes the euphoria of the time while everything was going so well, and the wheeling and dealing and conniving that went on. With the encouragement of the banks, he borrowed more money and increased his stake in the company. We all know what happened after the 1987 crash, but *Lost Property* provides a more personal view to the events and the bitterness that was to follow.

5 Ways to Save More Money on Your Mortgage
Martin Hawes

Payments on your mortgage are likely to be the biggest expense you have on your investment property. Consequently it is an area that you should be well versed in. There are big savings to be made when getting the right loan and Hawes' book gives you excellent mortgage knowledge and advice on how to approach this extremely important area.

The book is primarily aimed at home owners, but Hawes has a section for property investors and says that the main principles still apply. It gives you information on yield curves, loan tables and strategies; however, it also provides advice on how to approach the bank with the best chance of negotiating a successful result.

Residential Landlording for the Absolute Beginner
Harry Lawson

Lawson is a seasoned investor, editor of the Hawkes Bay Property Investors Association magazine, and a past president of the New Zealand Property Investors Federation.

His book is a very personal view of how investing in property works. It is written in a simple and easily understood manner, providing the advice that the author has gained from over 25 years in the industry.

Lawson believes that every journey or adventure in life, however serious or businesslike, should be tempered with a sense of humour and fun — he says that property is no exception.

About the Authors

Lisa Dudson

Lisa's keen interest in finance and investment began with the purchase of a New Zealand share portfolio when she was 16. She is now a certified financial planner who manages her own successful investment advisory business, Acumen Financial Planning Ltd. Her earlier career was in sales and marketing in the IT industry, predominantly in London.

Lisa is the vice-president of the New Zealand Property Investors Federation, vice-president of the Auckland Property Investors Association and secretary of the Auckland Financial Planners & Insurance Advisors Association.

She runs a number of courses on investment and property investment, coaches property investors through her business, regularly writes investment articles and has spoken on investing to a number of organisations. Lisa is passionate about property investment as a vehicle for creating wealth, has been investing in property for over 10 years and owns a number of properties in the North Island.

Andrew King

Andrew has had a love of property since childhood, saving for and purchasing his first investment property by the age of 24. He has always managed his own properties and enjoys this aspect of being a property investor.

His passion for the industry led him to developing the *Auckland Landlord* newsletter in 1996, which provided current and independent information to Auckland property investors. The newsletter grew into the national publication, *Residential Property Investor* magazine.

Andrew has been a long-term committee member of the Auckland Property Investors Association, and is its current president.

Andrew has spoken at property investment seminars and written for several magazines and newspapers, including the *New Zealand Herald* and *Sunday Star Times*. He has appeared on the television programme *Money Matters* and is often sought by radio stations and other media to share his knowledge on property investment matters.

Lisa Dudson and Andrew King offer a mentoring service aimed at tailoring their property investment knowledge to you personally. This involves goal setting, strategies, setting up the right structure, finance and more.

You can contact Lisa on (09) 360 3256
or Andrew on (09) 815 8642
or visit their website at: www.propertyinvestor.info/guide
